Strong Women Series Book 4

Valencina, the Ivory Woman

Mary Jo Nickum

Saguaro Books, LLC
SB
Arizona

Saguaro Books, LLC
16845 E. Avenue of the Fountains, Ste. 325
Fountain Hills, AZ 85268
www.saguarobooks.com

ISBN: 9798863073750
Library of Congress Cataloging Number
LCCN: 2024934934
Printed in the United States of America
First Edition

Other Books by Mary Jo Nickum

Strong Women Series
A Girl Named Mary Book 1
Eve, The First [*Liberated*] Woman Book 2
Thecla, the First Woman Evangelist Book 3

The Aquitaine Reluctant Reader Series
Looking at the Cat; an Eye on Evolution Book 1
The Coelacanth; the Greatest Fish Story Ever Told
Book 2
Who Was Macho B and What We Know about
Jaguars Book 3
Fire in the Trees Book 4
The Making of the Grand Canyon Book 5
The California Condor, "The Big Ugly" Book 6
Deserts of the World Book 7
Climate Change Book 8

Chapter Book
Mom's Story, a Child Learns about MS

Dedication

This book is dedicated to readers who enjoy reading of historical female characters who have shaped the times during their lives and of future generations.

Valencina

Prologue

How the Ivory Man Became the Ivory Woman

No sex changes, no hormone treatments, no surgery, no therapy...nothing like that, not in 2500 BC. Sorry to disappoint you, readers, but those current strategies never occurred to these people or, if it did, there was no possibility of it being accomplished. This change occurred because it was the result of a mistake of identity. Yes, even learned researchers make mistakes. They made the same mistake as others have by using time-honored criteria for judging the sex of a skeleton based on the burial goods accompanying it. When encountering unusual, hard-to-come-by, elaborate or precious goods, the skeleton must have been important in his society. Of course if he was important, he must have been a leader and, if he was a leader, he must have been male, right? So went the logic for so long.

Enter a new technique that can identify an individual's sex based on tooth enamel. This process can be more effective than DNA analysis when studying remains in especially poor condition. Previous examination of the skeleton's poorly preserved pelvis had suggested the remains were of a man, but amelogenin peptide analysis of the tooth enamel detected the AMELX gene, which is located on the X chromosome. "This analysis told us precisely that the skeleton was female," said García Sanjuán of the University of Seville. Buried between 3,200 and 2,200 years ago with an ivory tusk, flint, an ostrich eggshell, amber, and a rock crystal dagger, the woman is now thought to have been the leader of her community because she had been buried alone. Most of the Copper Age burials in the region contain commingled bones, Sanjuán explained. "When we compared the grave goods with our database [of more than 2,000 grave sites in the area], we can clearly see that this woman stood head and shoulders above other individuals in terms of wealth and social status," he added. Researchers also now think this area of the Iberian Peninsula was a central gathering place. "It makes sense that the Ivory Lady would be buried here," Sanjuán concluded. This shows the researchers have shed the previous line of thought and are willing to entertain the results of their studies.

Valencina

The new scientific technique developed is based on the analysis of sexually dimorphic amelogenin peptides in tooth enamel by Nano flow liquid chromatography-tandem mass spectrometry. This new procedure can provide highly reliable sex determinations even for poorly preserved human skeletons. The application of this technique to prehistoric human remains has yielded results that are likely going to significantly modify the way gender archaeology will be approached in the future. By coupling proteomics with other recently developed scientific methods, such as isotopic and aDNA analysis, which are themselves expanding rapidly, the study of prehistoric social organization is set to change.

All this means the highest ranked person in Iberian Copper Age society was a woman. In addition, the lack of grave goods in infant burials suggests, in this period, individuals were not granted high status by birth rite. The authors, therefore, suggest the Ivory Woman achieved her status through merit and achievements in life.

Chapter 1

Valencina's Birth

In a place known to few, a woman was in labor. Two friends attended her as they awaited the birth of the woman's child. At last, the baby made its appearance—a girl. The infant howled as one of the attendants washed her tiny, warm body in the cool water of the underground river. The other attendant bathed the mother in the river. The mother was grateful for the cool bath. When bathed and dressed, she reclined on a matt to enjoy the cool temperature and nurse her new daughter. The temperature of the underground cave and river was a nearly constant 68° F, a most welcome reprieve from the desert temperature above ground.

Nickum

The river flowed on as the women arose and prepared to return home. "This is a perfect place for birthing a child," Rosina, the mother, said.

"Yes, we found it last year and we were overwhelmed with the coolness and the river under all this rock," the first friend said.

"And when your time was near, Ebeth and I decided to bring you here for the birthing," the second friend said.

"Debora, thanks to you and Ebeth, the birthing was a wonderful experience. Now we'll go home so the world can greet our precious girl baby," Rosina said.

They followed the trail to reach the surface and take the one mile trip back to the village. Upon arriving home, Rosina found her husband, Xennis, returned from his hunting trip, wondering where she was.

"I was hoping nothing happened to you, Rosina, although there was no sign of a marauding party," Xennis said.

"No," Rosina said, "no marauding party, unless you consider labor and two friends to help with birthing a raid," Rosina said, smiling as she handed the baby to Xennis, with care.

"My beautiful daughter, Rosina. You did a wonderful job to bring our daughter to life. I love you and her."

"Oh, Xennis, I love you too. I'm going to rest now and let her rest, too."

"All right, but have you thought of a name for her?"

"No, I haven't. Let's discuss it when I get up from my rest."

"All right, we'll do it then."

"It sounds as if you have some ideas for names."

"Yes, I do but it can wait until after your rest, which you have earned."

With a kiss they parted, the baby already asleep.

"Rosina, you're awake," Xennis said.

"Yes, the baby woke me up. She was hungry so I nursed her and she went back to sleep," Rosina said. "It's time for our evening meal."

"Yes, it'll be dark soon. This day is almost done."

"What are you cooking on the fire?"

"Oh, you noticed," Xennis said, chuckling. "I thought we could have some deer steaks from the hunt."

"A fine idea, Xennis. I'll get the wild carrots, onions and celery ready. Is there a space for bread on the fire?"

"Sure is, I'll just move the steaks forward a bit."

"We'll have a wonderful meal."

The bread was baked and all was ready for the meal. Xennis and Rosina ate in silence as they were famished. When finished eating, Xennis said "Let's name our baby girl."

"All right, Xennis but why are you insisting on naming her so soon? We're not sure she'll survive."

"Oh, she'll survive. I've never seen a healthier baby."

"I didn't know you were a judge of such things."

"I'm not qualified as a healer but I just feel she'll be alive after us."

"Feel it in your bones?"

"Yes, you could say that."

With that they convulsed into laughter.

After recovering, Rosina said, "You have an idea for a name?"

"Yes, I offer 'Valencina'," he said.

"Xennis, that's a beautiful name. Did you hear that somewhere?"

"Yes, a member of our hunting party said he wanted to name his daughter that but his wife said, 'No". I liked it, so, I thought if we had a daughter, I want to name her Valencina."

"I like the name, as well. Valencina it is."

"That was settled quickly. Now it's dark. I'll bank the fire and we can go to sleep for the night. Valencina will probably wake us up more than once," Xennis said, laughing.

"That's for certain. We have to sleep while she's sleeping."

"I don't know about sleeping like a baby. I haven't been a baby for a long time."

"Neither have I, but we're going to have to get used to it."

Valencina

Valencina awoke only once, Rosina nursed her and both went back to sleep almost immediately. Xennis did not awaken.

Chapter 2
Valencina Approaches Three Summers

Valencina was an active child. She learned to walk when just over one Summer. Rosina had a hard time keeping track of her while attempting to do all the tasks of a mother and wife. One day when Rosina was busy preparing hides for clothing, she realized she hadn't seen or heard from Valencina in some time. She looked around their house and asked her friend, Ebeth, if she'd seen Valencina.

"Yes," Ebeth said, "she was playing hunting with my boys."

"Where are they now?" asked Rosina.

"I'm not sure. They were here just a little time ago."

"We'd better look for them; Valencina is too young to go too far."

"All right, let's go. I'm concerned too."

They walked through the village, asking people they'd met if they'd seen the children. No one had. Rosina and Ebeth became more concerned as they walked. "The only other place the children could have gone is to the forest," Rosina said.

"I was hoping they didn't go there. There are all sorts of wild animals there," Ebeth said.

"They're taking the hunting seriously, I guess."

"Indeed, they are," agreed Ebeth.

As they approached the forest, Rosina and Ebeth began calling the children's names. They received no response.

"I didn't ask but did they have weapons?" Rosina asked.

"Well, yes and no," Ebeth confessed.

"What do you mean?" Rosina asked in alarm.

"They had bows and arrows made for their size by their father. They had extras so Valencina had a bow and arrows too," Ebeth said.

"Oh my," Rosina said. "That means Valencina is in on this hunting venture with full force. Have they been in the forest before?"

"Yes, the boys go with their father often. Valencina has not, I don't think."

"She's never mentioned it to me, if she has," Rosina said, her alarm growing.

Valencina

They walked into the forest, calling the children's names. After a while, they decided to sit and rest. Suddenly, they heard a rustling in the bushes and one of the boys emerged. "Why are you calling us and disturbing the hunt, Mother?" he asked, almost in a whisper.

"We were worried when you children disappeared," Ebeth said.

"We are not children, we are hunters," the boy said, with emphasis.

"Hunters tell their family they're going and for how long they expect to be gone," Ebeth said.

"I didn't know Father did that," the boy said.

"Well now you do. Where are the others? Ebeth asked, trying to be patient.

"They are spread out, trying to drive an animal to me, I'm on a stand, prepared to shoot it when it comes by," the boy said.

Rosina could remain quiet no longer. "Where is Valencina?" she asked.

"I'm not sure," the boy said. "She wanted to climb a ridge to see if any animals were there."

"How would she know? She might not see them," Rosina said.

"She wouldn't have to see them. She'd be looking for tracks," he said.

"How does she know about tracks?" Rosina said.

"She asked my father and he and her father showed her tracks and told her what they were," he said.

"Oh my, I had no idea she was so advanced," Rosina said. *I'll have a talk with Xennis when he gets home*, she thought.

Finally, one by one, the children came through the trees. Valencina was last, to Rosina's relief.

On their way home, Rosina asked Valencina how she learned to shoot an arrow.

"Like this, Mother," she said, proudly, expertly knocking the arrow and shooting the arrow into the distance.

"My goodness, Valencina, who taught you that?"

"Father did some and the boys and their father helped," Valencina said.

"They did a good job," Rosina admitted. *I really have to talk to Xennis.*

They arrived home in time to start the evening meal. Xennis arrived soon after them.

"Why so quiet? No one is talking or chattering," he observed.

"We have to talk," Rosina said, just above a whisper.

"Something wrong?" Xennis asked, in his usual bantering voice.

"Not now," Rosina said, whispering.

Valencina came into the house, breathless, saying "Father, I went hunting with the boys today."

"You did?" Xennis asked, encouraging her to tell all. Rosina rolled her eyes.

"Yes, I borrowed a bow and arrow and the boys and I went into the forest. I went up on the ridge and saw some tracks of a wild boar. I knew I couldn't shoot it, so I started down and Mother was sitting on a log with Ebeth, talking."

"You saw boar tracks?" Rosina asked, dismayed.

"Don't you worry, Rosina, she did the right thing. She came down right away," Xennis said.

"She shouldn't have gone into the forest anyway. Certainly not without telling anybody," Rosina said.

"You didn't tell anyone, Valencina?" Xennis asked.

"I thought the boys told their mother," Valencina said, with innocence

"Apparently they didn't. You broke the first rule of hunting, Valencina. You must always tell your family when you go hunting and where you're going and plan to get back," Xennis said, firmly but following it with a hug and a kiss. The hug and kiss resulted in instant dismissal of the impending tears.

"Is that what you wanted to talk about, Rosina?"

"That's only part of it. We'll talk later."

Talk, they did. The evening meal completed and Valencina gone to sleep, Rosina and Xennis sat before the fire. Xennis started the conversation.

"What bothers you, Rosina? So quiet during the meal."

'Yes, I am wondering how much you and Ebeth's man have been teaching Valencina?"

"We've answered her questions about hunting."

"You failed to mention to me her interest in hunting."

"I didn't know you cared, since I am also responsible for her learning."

"Yes, you are but we should discuss what we're teaching her."

"Do you plan to tell me when you teach her to cook and sew?"

"Those are women's tasks; I thought you'd know I'm teaching her that."

"Oh, I see, hunting is man's work, so she shouldn't learn that?"

"That's not what I'm saying. I just worry when she disappears and I don't know what she's up to," Rosina's real worry came out, at last.

"Yes, I understand your concern and I think I've handled it with firmness and love."

"I think you handled it well, Xennis. I hope she took it to heart."

"I'm sure she will. She's smart and wants to be a part of life."

Little did either parent know it was Valencina's idea to go on the hunt; she wanted to lead a hunt.

With that, they banked the fire and returned to their sleeping mats.

Chapter 3

Valencina Reaches Eight Summers

Valencina awoke one spring morning, birds were singing and the sun was shining. The thunderstorm from last night had cleared and she was ready to meet the day. She was going fishing with the boys, her favorite companions. She'd fashioned a pole from a sapling nearby and used fine sinew from her mother's sewing kit to make the line. Now, all she had to do was get some worms to weave onto a bone hook her father had given her and she'd be ready to go. Digging the worms wasn't difficult today because the dirt was damp from the storm last night. All she had to do was scrape away a little top dirt and the worms were available. Valencina had a handful of worms, which she placed in a carrying bag, grabbed her pole and she was on her way to the local stream.

The boys she planned to meet were not there so she threaded a worm on the hook, put the line in the water and sat to wait. The pole jerked once with a slight nudge then the tip of the pole dropped into the water. Valencina grabbed the pole and gave it a strong upward jerk. Sure enough, a large bordallo fought for a time, but Valencina pulled the line and pole to the stream bank in a move of backing and lifting until the fish and pole tip were over the bank. Then she removed the hook and pushed a long stick through its gills, laid it on the bank to thrash until it died.

Valencina continued fishing for several hours. After she'd caught several more fish, brown trout and tench, she decided to take the fish home, clean them and offer them to her mother for the evening meal. When Valencina arrived home, she propped the pole against the house and sat to clean the fish using a bone knife. Fish cleaning was an easy job. She'd watched her father do it many times. After she finished, she took the fish into the house.

"Mother, here is our meal for tonight," Valencia said, with pride.

"Oh my, you caught all those?" Rosina asked. "Didn't the boys help you?"

"No, Mother; they never came so I caught them myself."

"I didn't know you knew how to fish all by yourself."

"It wasn't hard. I made the pole yesterday and grabbed one of Father's hooks, uncovered some worms this morning and I took it all to the stream and fished."

"That's very good; did you give your father back the hook?"

"I'll do it as soon as I clean it and take it off the pole."

"All right, now we have food for tonight. I'll get the vegetables ready and when your father gets here, he can start the fire."

"I'll start the fire, Mother."

"That's not necessary, Valencina. I don't want you starting the fire. It's too dangerous."

"Oh, Mother," Valencina sighed as she left the house.

Of course, Valencina wanted to start the fire, she'd watched her father do it every evening and this was the time she could start it to cook her fish. She piled sticks of wood on top of the dry leaves, ferns and kindling. Valencina picked up two stones, rubbed them together in a quick front to back motion to create a spark. As she leaned close to the pile of wood, the sparks caught the leaves and tinder. The fire was started. She was unaware her father was watching her.

"Well done, daughter," Xennis said.

"I didn't know you were watching," Valencina said. "I wasn't close enough to the wood when I created the first sparks."

"That's good you corrected your mistake without anyone helping."

"I don't think Mother wanted me to start the fire but I caught some fish today and I want to cook them."

"All right, do you know how to do that?"

"Yes, I've watched you many times. I'll put the green poles on top of the fire and set the fish on them to cook. I'll watch them so they don't burn."

"Sounds as if you've got it down well. I'll be inside if you need me."

"All right, I doubt I'll need any help."

"I doubt it, too," Xennis said, under his breath as he walked into the house.

The evening meal was ready and Valencina brought in the fish. Rosina had made bread earlier in the day and she fixed the vegetables in a cider sauce that complemented the fish. Xennis complemented Rosina and Valencina for the delectable meal.

"You women are excellent cooks," he said.

"Cooking the fish was almost as much fun as catching them," Valencina said.

"I'm proud of your cooking skill, Valencina," Rosina said.

"I have good teachers," she said, between mouthfuls.

"Good teachers are great, but you are able to put all that to good use. You'll make a fine wife and mother someday," Xennis said.

"I don't want to be a wife and mother," Valencina announced.

Valencina

"Is that so?" Xennis asked, with eyebrows raised. Rosina stopped chewing and raised her eyebrows too.

"Yes," Valencina said. "I want to be a leader. I want to hunt, fight battles and win wars."

"That's a hefty goal, Valencina," Xennis said.

"And not becoming of a woman," Rosina said, having swallowed her food and found her voice.

"A woman can do anything she wants to if she works hard and learns what's necessary to do it," Valencina said.

"You got it right, Valencina," Xennis said.

"Xennis, you are not making my job as a mother any easier. Don't encourage that kind of talk from your daughter," Rosina said.

"It's true, Rosina. She can be what she can be and do what she wants. She doesn't need our permission," Xennis said.

"I think she'll change her mind when she gets a little older," Rosina said.

Valencina stayed out of the discussion. Instead, she let her mind wander. *I will work with my father to get better at shooting arrows and maybe he'll let me learn to throw a spear. He already promised I could lead a hunting party, some day. Maybe, just maybe, he'll let me join him when he goes to war next time. Mother would be furious, though and she might be unhappy with me for a long time. Oh, well, I'll just have to keep trying to be a good hunter and warrior.*

Chapter 4

Valencina Reaches Twelve Summers

Xennis has told Valencina it is her turn to lead a hunting party. "Oh, Father," she said, "I've dreamed of that for so long. I'll get started right away."

"Calm down and approach it methodically," Xennis said.

"Don't worry, Father, I've watched you for a long time. I'll make sure all the men are ready, remember what we've agreed to hunt and they have the necessary weapons, especially spears."

"Good thinking, Valencina, this hunt will go well."

Valencina made her own preparations then proceeded to pass the message to the entire hunting party of six men, including her father. Her message stated: "We'll embark on a boar hunt in two days. Please bring rawhide thongs and at least one spear." This message was passed word-of-mouth to the entire hunting party. The party knew the hunt always began at sunup and usually involved at least two days. She knew she did not have to tell everyone to pack food for the overnight venture. Of course, it could be longer and, if so, more food would be necessary. If that happened, they'd kill rabbits or other wildlife to cook and eat.

Two suns later, Valencina was at her best. She dressed for the hunt as all the other hunters were dressed; hide shorts, hair tied at the nape of the neck with a leather thong and bare feet. She hoisted a bag containing food, leather thongs and arrows on her shoulders. She carried a spear several inches longer than she was tall in her right hand and her bow in her left. She was oh, so ready.

The party was gathered and all began trudging to the forest, Valencina in the lead. They walked a known trail and topped a rise in the forest, looking for boar tracks. No one saw any boar tracks until later in the day. The sun had long passed its zenith and shadows were growing long. They had reached level ground, without rocks but with a bubbling spring.

"It is growing late, too late for tracking. We must stop here for the night and begin again at first light. Keep your spears nearby. We'll eat now, drink from the spring and sleep. Tomorrow we'll begin our search for tracks again," Valencia announced.

No one questioned. The hunters were tired after a long hike and unfruitful search for tracks. They drank from the spring, unpacked their food and sat on the leaf strewn ground. Xennis, concerned about Valencia's mood, approached her before sitting on the ground.

"Glad you joined me, Father," Valencina said.

"I wanted to talk to you for a minute before the other men join us. You are doing a fine job of leading the hunt, even though we were unable to find tracks today," Xennis said.

"Thanks, Father. I am not in the least disheartened. I know this is the way of the hunt."

"Yes, and it could go on for several days."

"This I know. I am prepared."

"You are going to be a good leader, Valencina."

'Thank you, Father. My heart is in it."

At that time, the other men joined them to eat their meager food from their bags. They sat in a circle laughing between bites. After the food was consumed, the hunting chiding ended and one of the hunters spoke, looking directly at Valencina. "Valencina, you are a good leader. I feel we're in boar territory. It's just a matter of time."

"Thank you, we are, indeed in boar country. I've seen boar tracks on previous visits. They can't be far."

The other hunter joined in with similar accolades, though they'd seen no tracks. Valencina thought, *the rain washed the previous tracks away. I hope a boar doesn't come during the dark of night. It could be trouble, though it would be unusual. We've lit no fire, so animals should not be aware of our presence.*

Valencina awoke just as the dawn was breaking. She arose, relieved herself behind some bushes, went to the spring for water and returned to find several hunters beginning the same morning rituals. All the hunters ate their morning biscuits and discussed the morning hunt with Valencina. By the time they finished, it was full light, as the sun peaked over the horizon.

"We'll proceed down the hill and onto flat land where the trees are smaller and a stream runs along one side. Boars need water as do all animals. I think that is our best chance of seeing tracks in the semi wet soil, along the streambank," Valencina said.

"All right, let's do it," they said, in unison.

Loaded for the trip down the hill, resuming the search for boar tracks, they followed Valencina without question. Arriving at the streambank, the hunters saw a multitude of animal tracks, one over another. The tracks were so jumbled no one set of tracks seemed to be the most recent. "We'll walk along the streambank and look for boar tracks. I'm sure there will be some," Valencina said.

The hunting party began their search for tracks along the muddy stream bank. There were many tracks over each other, not discernable as to which came last. As they were bent looking for the tracks the sound of a rushing beast was felt rather than heard. Valencina stood and marched past the party as they stood looking past her. A boar was charging down an incline, as it was about to change coarse to come toward them, Valencina launched her spear. The spear struck the animal behind the right shoulder. Other spears came almost at the same time. The boar was dead. The hunters all wanted to know who had thrown the killing spear. They checked the animal over and all determined the spear into the heart, the one right behind the right shoulder killed the boar.

The hunters lauded Valencia for throwing the killing spear. One hunter exclaimed, "You, Valencina, our leader, killed the boar with one spear."

"Extraordinary," another hunter said.

"Amazing," said another.

Xennis said nothing, beaming with pride.

Valencina thanked them for their praise and said, "Now the hardest part is left to do. We must butcher the animal and haul it home."

At her direction, they all pulled their sharpened bone knives from their packs and went to work degutting, beheading and skinning the boar. The skin was peeled and saved for further processing and use. The meat was cut into large pieces and loaded into large sacks the hunters unfolded from their packs. Because the pieces were too heavy to carry, each hunter dragged a sack for the walk home. Valencina insisted on pulling her share of the meat, although the other hunters said, because she was the leader, she should not have to pull a sack. *They are just saying that because I'm a girl,* Valencina thought. *I'll show them how strong I am and how wrong they are.*

It was after dark when the hunting party made the long trek home. Everyone unrolled their sleeping mats and slept at Xennis and Valencina's place. There was an open, flat, grass filled area in front of the house, so the other hunters could sleep there, while Valencina and Xennis went into the house. They entered without speaking and went to their rooms for much needed sleep.

The next morning, Xennis and Valencina explained their success to Rosina and the front area full of awakening hunters. Valencina and Rosina hurried to prepare food for the rest of the hunters to break their fast. After all were satisfied, they divided the meat further so everyone had their share. The hide was given to Valencina and Xennis for leading a successful hunting trip. Valencina thought her father should take the hide but, he said "No, Valencina, it is yours. You deserve it all. You pulled it home with additional meat. You are a strong young woman."

"Thank you, Father, for that statement. I am proud to be your daughter," Valencina said. *Most important to me, he called me a 'young woman',* Valencina thought.

Valencina proceeded to begin work processing the hide. She spread it out on the ground in front of the house. "We can show you how to process the hide and help you. Ebeth can join us and make the work go faster," Rosina offered.

"Thanks, Mother, I can do it myself. I've listened to your discussions about processing hides. I'm well prepared to do the work."

"All right, Ebeth and I will leave you to your work," Rosina said, shrugging her shoulders.

Four suns later, Valencina stretched the hide on four poles anchored by thongs encircling tree stumps. There the hide would finish processing and dry. She'd then fold the hide for future use. *Perhaps it can be used for a new door covering, for windows or cut into pieces to be used as a sling for hauling fire wood or a larger piece to use for dragging larger sticks of wood. Smaller hide pieces would make good bags for other uses,* Valencina thought, with pride.

A season later, Valencina began to wonder what was beyond their settlement. *There must be other clans and other settlements. We've heard from none others for as long as I can remember. I asked Father, he just said there are others but we need to stay here and protect our settlement but when I asked him, protect our settlement from what, he just shrugged and continued working. I need to ask Rupert or one of the other council members.*

She decided to attend the next council meeting. The leader was old and frail. He spoke with a trembling voice that was hard to hear. He was held in high esteem because of his age. He was the oldest person Valencina had ever seen. She thought he might collapse at any moment. He didn't, he continued to babble, saliva dripping from his mouth. Valencina decided not to try to ask him about the excursion she had begun to plan. Instead, she asked her father and Rupert to talk with her after the meeting.

Valencina left the meeting as soon as she could, waiting outside under a tree for the meeting attendees to emerge. At last, some men began to leave. When almost all had left, two helping the Leader to walk to his house, Rupert and Xennis came out. She waved to them and they headed toward her. "Valencina, you left so fast, any particular reason?" asked her father.

"Yes, it was very difficult to understand the leader. He didn't sound as if he were able to talk well and follow the meeting," Valencina said.

"We can understand him because he's been our leader for almost his entire life," Rupert said.

"Since he was a boy?" Valencina asked, with incredulity.

"Almost. He was the leader when I joined the council," Xennis said.

"He became leader after we settled here nearly 40 summers ago," Rupert said.

"That is an incredibly long time," Valencina said.

"What do you wish to talk to us about, Valencina?" Xennis asked.

"I was hoping to ask at council but the leader didn't look as if he'd understand my question," replied Valencina.

"Well, let's see if we can help," Rupert said.

"I have been wondering what is beyond us? There must be more clans. If so, what are they doing? Are they similar to us?" Valencina said.

"Those are good questions. We stay to ourselves so we won't provoke our neighbors into raiding or mistaken us for initiating a raid," Xennis said. Rupert nodded in agreement.

"Well, that sounds to be a narrow assessment of the idea," she said. "Has no one ever explored the surrounding area? I mean beyond the forest and the plain? Hasn't anybody ever wondered who else is out there?"

"I think we've just been busy staying alive, feeding ourselves and raising our children," Rupert said.

"I am suggesting we get the council to gather an exploratory group together to traverse the forest, the plain and beyond to find what else is there," Valencina said.

"That may not be as easy as you think, Valencina. Most of this clan is comfortable here with no raiding parties in many moons," Xennis said.

"If we stay here saying the same thing over and over, we'll never know," Valencina said, voice rising with insistence.

"Well, Xennis, Valencina seems determined to follow her line of thinking.

Perhaps, we could bring it forward in the next council meeting," Rupert said.

"I don't know, Rupert, We might be run out of the meeting with such a suggestion, Xennis said, in all seriousness.

"Do you really think the council members are that stuck in the present?" Valencina asked.

"Yes, Valencina, I do" Xennis answered.

"Would you be willing to lead such a group, Valencina?" Rupert asked.

"Yes, I certainly would," Valencina stated.

"All right, Valencina, here is what I'm thinking. Xennis and I will talk to a few other high ranking council members about the general idea. You spend some time deciding on where you plan to go, how to get there, what supplies you'd need, how big the group should be and when to start. If you can come up with all that, we will see if any other council members will side with us when we bring it forward," Rupert said.

Valencina was heartened by Rupert's response. It sounded as if he really were interested in 'the beyond'. She was concerned her father looked unable to understand what she wanted to do and why. She'd always thought her father was more forward thinking and not stuck in going along with the current thought. For the first time, she thought of him as being an obstruction to moving the clan forward. *Maybe, that thinking is why such a senile leader is still in power. He shouldn't be in power. Could he be replaced? How...*

Valencina

I'm not going to think about that now. I must think about leading a group of explorers. Who will it be, I hope they're young, like me and not old and stuffy in their way of thinking. I can't believe even my father fits in that group. Well, I'll start by asking Rupert and Ebeth's sons if they'd be interested in joining me. I have to work on some of the other things Rupert mentioned first.

First of all, where would we go? I think we should go toward the rising sun? Why? I don't know. Second, how will we get there? Walk and maybe drag hides loaded with tents and supplies. We need dried meat, flour to make biscuits, we can collect vegetables, berries and nuts along the way. We can also hunt along the way. Everyone should have at least one pair of new foot coverings and enough clothes to make the trip. Sleeping mats, cook ware and drinking vessels are also necessary.

I think the group should be at least six, maybe as many as ten. We must keep it small, though; we don't want to look or act as a raiding party.

When to leave...I think, early summer when the water in the rivers and streams has abated after the winter thaw. That gives us time to plan, prepare for the journey and convince the older council members of the value of looking beyond our fortifications. I wonder if that is possible. I'll go to Ebeth to see if her sons have time to talk.

Valencina approached Ebeth's door, stood outside and asked "Is anyone home?"

"Yes, I'm here," Ebeth said. "I haven't seen you for a long time."

"I know, Ebeth. I've had many chores and work with Mother. She's not feeling well," Valencina said.

"I thought she looked thinner and walked with a serious limp."

"Yes, she fell and, I think broke something. She is in much pain. She drinks several cups of willow bark tea every day."

"That's probably not good for her but I don't know of anything else she could do for pain."

"She doesn't either. It hurts her when she sits. Lying on the sleeping mat then getting up, is impossible for her. Father made her something with poles joined close together attached to the roof with leather straps. The poles are covered by straw or dry grass to make it soft."

"I see. That way she doesn't have to get up and down on the floor. Your father is quite creative."

"Yes, he cares for Mother so much. She stays on the poles almost all the time."

"That's sad. How are you doing, Valencia?"

"I am doing quite well. Are Timus and Edecón home?"

"They've both gone into the forest to hunt squirrels for the evening meal."

"I want to talk to them about a plan I have."

Valencina

"All right. I'll tell them you were here and I'll send them over to you when they get back. It shouldn't be too long."

"Thanks, Ebeth."

"Thanks for stopping by, Valencina, and tell your mother I'll stop over soon."

"All right, Ebeth, she'll welcome you."

Valencina went home to tell her mother about Ebeth and to begin preparations for the evening meal, baking bread was the first chore to be accomplished.

Valencina had just placed a loaf of bread in the oven when Timus and Edecón walked around the edge of the round house.

"Valencina, my mother said you wanted to talk to us," Timus said.

"Yes, do you have time to listen to a plan I have?"

"Sure, what kind of a plan?" Timus asked.

"Come over here. Let's sit under this tree and I'll tell you the plan that is in my head right now."

She told them about the council meeting, the aged leader, her discussion with her father and their father then she told them of her plan as far as she'd thought it out.

"That's quite a plan, Valencina," smiled Edecón

"How will we know we've gone far enough?" asked Timus, always the more practical one.

"When we've found something, anything different from what we have or what we're doing," Valencina said.

"I can see why Father was willing to think about such an idea. He is the adventurous one. He's always disappointed when the hunting ends too soon. He says it's not any fun when you don't see anything new," Edecón said.

"Should we ask him to join us?" Valencina asked.

"Not yet. I think Mother would be against his going when we don't know what's out there," Timus said.

"Will she let you come?" Valencia asked.

"We won't ask her. If Father says we can go, that's all we need," Edecón said. "It sounds to be the kind of adventure he would endorse."

"All right let's talk about it tomorrow and think of who else might want to join us," Valencina said.

All right, we'll be over after everything we have to do is done," Timus said and Edecón nodded his head with vigor.

They continued to meet every few suns, as their time allowed. Valencina was busier because she'd taken on most of the housework for her ailing mother. Ebeth helped when she could and assured Valencina she would look after her mother if they decided to go afar soon. Valencina doubted it would be soon, in that several council members seemed to question the validity of such a trip. Valencina begged her father to propose some time at the next council meeting for her to speak about her plans and what she hoped to accomplish. Xennis agreed to speak to Rupert about it because he also had two sons planning to go on the explorative trip. Valencina felt comfortable with her father's angle because Rupert had been supportive so far.

Valencina, Timus and Edecón invited two more people about their age, Lagunas and Daleninar. Valencina didn't think it was enough. She wanted at least seven but, if five was all they could find willing to take on the work of travel and the possible hardships involved, she was willing to take only five.

"Think about it this way, Valencina," Lagunas said, "we are willing to take on whatever challenges we meet. We all know each other quite well. If we take on more, especially if we don't know them as well or don't trust them as much, we'd be asking for trouble. We know the skills and capabilities of each other. I can't think of any others with whom I'd feel this comfortable."

"Well said, Lagunas," Timus said. "We have to be able to trust each other with our lives. We don't know what we might be up against."

"All right, I understand what you are saying. Yes, trust is an important quality we must all feel for each other. Does everyone feel they can trust the others with their lives?"

She heard an emphatic "Yes" from the entire group. "All right, I heard you. I think the group is large enough to protect each other from any wild animals we might come to and small enough so we won't be considered a raiding party," Valencina said.

"Maybe a scouting party," Edecón said, laughing. The others joined him laughing at his joke.

"Now, let's think about things we might need, other than food," Valencina said, "especially think about past, longer hunting trips. What did we forget to bring that we ended up needing? What did we use more of than we planned? What did we take along we didn't use or need?"

Much mumbling between neighbors became a group discussion led by Valencina. "All right, I think we have a sense of what we all need. Let's end this discussion today and everyone return to their homes and begin to make a stack of items you think you'll need. Be sure to consider weight, purpose and need of each item. Ask each other if you are unsure. Please ask questions about the utility of an item if you are not sure. I'll let you know when we will meet again."

After having met once, Valencina called an emergency meeting. When they'd all arrived, Valencina started to talk without a preamble of greeting. "I am going to speak at the next council meeting in three suns. The council leader is too sick to run the meeting, so Rupert will be the head of the council."

"That's our father," Edecón stated, with pride, looking sideways at Timus.

"Yes and he has been supportive of our venture," Valencina said.

"Why is this important? Daleninar asked.

Valencina

"Daleninar and anyone else who doesn't realize it, we need the support from the council to give our venture standing," Valencina explained. "The council needs to know where we're going and why. They need to know we are traveling in peace. If we are accused of raiding, they'll know it is a mistake and come to our defense. If we don't arrive back here in twenty-four moons, they'll know we are in trouble and can form a search party. Of course, we don't want these things to happen but it is appropriate to have these people know and support our plans."

"Who will present the plan? Will you?" asked Timus.

"Yes, I will present the plan. As many of you should attend the meeting as can spare the time, not to talk but perhaps meet the council members after the meeting and, maybe, answer questions."

Valencina then proceeded to tell them how she planned to address the council, giving as much detail as possible. Of course, she couldn't give minute detail because they didn't know all the facets of their encounters. After her delivery, they agreed she had presented all they knew and no one had any suggestions for changes.

At last, the day arrived for the council meeting. Valencina was ready. She kissed her mother and left for the meeting. When she arrived, the council was ready to begin. Rupert stood to open the meeting. "Our guest speaker has arrived. She has an interesting message we all need to hear. "Valencina, please stand to address the council," Rupert said, taking his chair.

"Good afternoon, council members and guests," Valencina began, "thank you for giving me this time to present our plan to explore the lands to the east of here. Five of us, all about the same number of summers, are planning an expedition to the east and northeast. We want to know who is out there, where they live, what resources are there, how they use them and how they live. This will give us the opportunity to learn from others in peaceful surroundings. The five members of our group are seasoned hunters, familiar with living in the forest or on the plain. We have learned to use bows, arrows, slings and spears to hunt and defend ourselves. We only expect to use them for hunting. We want to live with a settlement of people to learn their ways and learn useful skills to bring back to our settlement. We plan to be gone for no more than twenty-four moons. We beg you to give us time at a council meeting upon our return to give you the information we have received from our stay with these peoples. Thank you for listening to our plan," Valencina said, taking her seat.

Rupert rose and said, "Thank you for such an ambitious plan. It gives us much to discuss and think about. Because all the members of the group are here, I will close the meeting at this time and give the council members the opportunity to ask questions of these young adventurers. We will discuss this plan at the next council meeting in seven suns."

Valencina

Four or five council members stood in a line to talk to Valencina. She noticed the rest of the council members each chose a different group member to whom to talk.

Valencina received the first council member, a woman who began by asking, "Who came up this plan?"

"I did," Valencina stated. "I have wondered what was beyond where we hunted for many moons."

"Are you unhappy here?" the woman asked.

"Oh no, I'm wondering what else and who else is out there."

"That's interesting. Maybe you don't have enough to occupy your hands or mind."

"That is incredible you'd say that. We all have much to do at home. There is much work."

"Well, maybe that's it. This is your chance to get away from the work."

"I'm sorry you see our plan in such a dim light."

Stepping to the side, Valencina said, "I'll talk to the next person," Another council member stepped forward.

"Valencina, thank you for telling us about your ambitious plan. It sounds as if you've thought it out and understand what you've set yourselves out to accomplish. I will be ready to listen to all the information you bring back. I think it will be exciting. I wish I was young, I'd want to go with you."

"That is a reassuring comment, sir. I'm looking forward to meeting new people and learning new skills."

The council member stepped away and another took his place. The rest had similar comments with almost no questions. *I wonder what the others are hearing. I hope it's nothing like that first council member. I'll ask them as soon as we get away from here,* thought Valencina.

A short time later, Valencina met her group and they moved to sit under a grouping of trees. "Let's just sit here and breathe the fresh air. The meeting house was hot and I felt dizzy," Valencina said.

"What do you think, Valencina?" Timus asked.

"I was going to ask you the same, Timus. I think they will agree to our exploration. I know my father will speak in favor."

"I'm sure our father will speak in favor," Edecón said.

"Was any one confronted with objections?" Valencina asked.

"Only some with questions that were unknown at this time," Daleninar said.

"What were some of those?" Valencina asked Daleninar.

"'How far can you get in a sun?' 'What if you meet a strange animal you've never seen before?' 'Are you going to cross any large waters?'" Daleninar said.

"All right, it sounds as if they're puzzled. Their discussions with the other members will help. I'll tell my father about the questions so he can discuss them if the questions come up," Valencina said.

"All in all, Valencina, I think it went well. You are a good speaker," Lagunas said.

"Thanks everybody for coming to the meeting and talking to individual council members. Let's go home and think about the meeting and our trip," Valencina said. "It might help to discuss it with our parents, too," Valencina said, in an after-thought.

Seven suns later, Rupert opened the meeting with the intention of voting for or against the trip plan Valencina had provided at the last meeting. Valencina was expecting a difficult discussion with vitriol from some members, especially the woman who accosted her after the meeting. To her surprise, the vote was not close; only two members voted 'no', all the others voted in the affirmative. *There must have been some lively discussions during the time before this meeting for so many to support it*, thought Valencina.

After a few more meeting items, Rupert asked Valencina to come forward. Valencina had no idea Rupert was about to make an announcement. "Valencina, our Leader has given me the powers of leadership of the clan and the gods we honor. Our Leader asks me to bestow on you the title of Honorary Clan Leader and Leader of Worship. In his stead, I give you these honors. Please carry them with you but do not require special treatment because of them."

Valencina remained standing, head bowed deep. She was overcome by the depth and expanse of the honors.

Rupert placed drops of holy oil on her head, her hands and her feet. "Serve the clan well and your honors will be for life," Rupert said.

Through tears, Valencina invoked the Sun god for success of their venture to better the clan.

I'll mention this honor to no one, Valencina thought, as she left the council hall. *It could cause an impediment to comradery, which is an important quality of the group for this trip into the unknown.*

On her walk home, Valencia was overcome by a feeling of foreboding. She had never felt such an intense dread before. She hastened her steps toward home. She was sure something was wrong. She pushed past the hide drape at the door and hurried to her mother's bed. Her mother appeared to be sleeping and Valencia said, "I'm home, mother." That statement would often cause Rosina to stir. Nothing. "Mother?" asked Valencina. Still nothing. Valencina bent to kiss her mother and her lips met a cold forehead. She jumped back, startled. *Oh, no Mother is dead. I need to go to Ebeth now,* thought Valencina.

Valencina asked for entrance and Ebeth welcomed her. "What is the matter, Valencina?"

"I just got home. I leaned over to kiss Mother and her forehead was cold," Valencina answered, eyes filling with tears.

"Oh, Valencina, that is terrible news. I visited her late this morning. She was groggy but able to recognize me and drink some water."

"She's been ill for so long, Ebeth. I knew this would happen but I always thought I'd be near when it did," Valencina said, sobbing now.

"Yes, Valencina, we always want to be near someone we love when the end comes but the exact time is never known. Come, let us go back to your house and be there when your father arrives."

"All right, he'll be home soon."

They had just entered the house when Xennis said, "I just saw you come in. What's going on?"

"Father, it's terrible; Mother is dead," Valencina said as she erupted in tears again."

"Rosina is dead?" Xennis asked, in disbelief, looking at Ebeth as he held Valencina. Ebeth was nodding in affirmation.

"Let me go to her," he said, releasing Valencina and walking to Rosina's bed. He slipped his arm beneath her shoulder, hugged her and kissed her. Then he returned to the women. "Yes, she is dead. This means we'll have to proceed with internment. I will see to the place and time, I must ask you to assist by preparing the body," Xennis said.

"We will do that, Xennis" Ebeth said, just above a whisper.

With her arms across Valencia's shoulders, Ebeth moved toward the door, stepping out with care and crossing the road to her house.

Two days later, Rosina was laid in her tomb. A rock was placed at the opening as was every grave, where future bodies will be interred. Valencina left with Xennis, Ebeth and Rupert after they'd said their final words to Rosina. Ebeth and Rupert invited them to stay for the rest of the day, into the evening until everyone would seek sleep.

Chapter 5
Valencina Passes Sixteen Summers

The winter came and Valencina took over the housekeeping, cooking and cleaning. She did her best to look after her father, who she knew missed her mother to the depth of his heart. He talked little and was away most of the time. He joined hunting parties and drinking parties. Xennis seemed to do anything he could so as to be home as little as possible. Valencina knew he was not avoiding her, he just missed Rosina. She, though, was not able to discern how to help him.

Because she did the house work, it didn't mean she wasn't preparing for the exploratory trip in the spring. Valencina met with her team, at least once every seven suns. Winter was drawing to a close as the first buds of some of the bushes opened. *We'll have just one or two meetings before it is time to leave,* Valencina thought, as she prepared to leave for this meeting.

As was the usual meeting place, under a large pine tree in the center of the settlement, Valencina arrived to find Lagunas and Daleninar waiting for the others.

"Good sun, friends," Valencina said.

"Good sun. All is well with us," Daleninar said.

"Welcome, Timus and Edecón," Valencina said, as they were the last to arrive.

"Now, we're all together. We must take a last look at our list to be sure we have everything and to make sure nothing has been left off," Valencina said.

"We have the necessary bows and arrows," Timus said, as Edecón nodded with vigor.

"Do we need spears?" Valencina said.

"They might be useful for protection but it might make us look as if we're expecting to raid," Lagunas said.

"That's right. We are not a raiding party and we don't want to look to be one. I'm thinking of our security," Valencina said.

"We would only use spears if we encounter a boar or something that big," Lagunas said.

"I don't think we will encounter anything that large if we make enough noise in the forest," Daleninar said.

"We can count on you, Daleninar, to make noise," Edecón said, teasing.

After everyone recovered from laughing, Valencina asked them to help make the decision. "All those who want to take spears, raise their hands," Valencina said.

Two hands went up, Timus and Edecón.

"Everyone else does not want spears?" asked Valencina. The others, including Valencina raised their hands and nodded.

"All right, that settles it. No spears," Valencina said. "Next, we must discuss food and water for the beginning of the trip."

"I'll make loaves of bread for the trip," Daleninar volunteered.

"I'll pack dried meat. How much should I pack?" Lagunas asked.

"Let's plan on one moon's worth," Valencina said.

"I'll arrange a hunting party so we'll have fresh meat," Lagunas said. "Timus and Edecón, will you join me?"

"I'll join you too," Daleninar said.

"So will I," Valencina said.

Everyone convulsed in laughter again.

"Now the hunting party is settled. Nothing in the forest is safe now," Valencina said, working hard not to laugh. After she finished, they all laughed again. Daleninar was wiping tears from her eyes with all the laughter.

"We'll meet again after the hunt. Lagunas will decide on the time for the hunt," Valencina said.

"Let's hunt two suns from now," Lagunas said.

Everyone agreed and they all arose and left for their homes.

Two days later, the hunting party assembled, led by Lagunas. Everyone carried a bow and a shoulder pack of arrows.

"We'll head for the forest where the pines are thickest; the needles covering the ground will help us to be extra quiet," Lagunas said.

"Daleninar and I will circle to the left and approach your stand, while Edecón circles to the right and drives from the right. We'll not need to be as quiet so the deer will advance in front of us toward Lagunas and Timus," Valencina said.

"That is how I see it. Timus and I will sit close to the meadow line, about twenty sticks into the forest," Lagunas said.

Everyone nodded their heads in agreement, picked up bows and shouldered their packs and trudged off in their agreed directions.

An hour later, Valencina, Daleninar and Edecón arrived at the stand. Lagunas and Timus each had shot a deer and were beginning to gut them.

"Looks as if you were both successful," Valencina said, in greeting.

"Yes we were. First Timus shot his and mine came from another direction," Lagunas said.

"That's wonderful," Daleninar said. "Now we'll have plenty of meat for the trip."

"We'll carry it to Lagunas' home and Timus' home then we'll prepare it to dry," Valencina said.

They piled the chunks of meat on the deer skins and drug them out of the forest. It was slow work and the sun was well past its zenith when they arrived at their individual homes. Daleninar and Lagunas worked on Lagunas' deer and Timus and Edecón worked on Timus' kill. Valencina decided to go home to see if her father was there. *I need to find out if Father is home and all right. I worry about him. He seems to have lost interest in home and me. I wonder what is wrong with him. Maybe he's in pain and doesn't want to talk about it,* she thought. When she approached the door, she called, "Father, are you home?"

"I'm here but I can't do much," came a soft answer.

Valencina quickened her steps into the house. "Father, what is the matter?" she asked.

"I have such a pain here," he said, pointing to the left side of his chest and down his left arm.

"I'll go to talk to Ebeth to see if she can help."

"Don't tell her. She'll tell Rupert and he'll want to come over. Everyone will know I'm weak."

"Father, that's not important, getting help is important. Rupert and Ebeth care about you. There's no shame in that. They know how strong you are."

"Not now. Go," Xennis said, waving a weak hand.

Valencina approached Ebeth who was outside gathering nuts from one of the trees.

"Ebeth, my father is in pain and I need you to see him. Can you come back with me?"

"Yes, I'll set these nuts in the house and I'll be right with you."

They entered the house and they saw Xennis lying on the floor.

"Father, why are you on the floor?" Valencina asked.

No response.

"Father," she said touching his shoulder.

Still no response.

"Let me see if I can awaken him," Ebeth said.

She received no reply either. Then she listened to his chest. She heard no breathing or heartbeat. "I believe he's dead, Valencina."

"Oh, he was alive just a few minutes ago," Valencina said, tears forming in her eyes.

"Was he complaining of pain?"

"Yes, in his chest and left arm."

"Was he sitting here?"

"Yes," Valencina said between sobs.

"All right, Valencina. I think his heart was hurting. He probably tried to stand and fell, possibly hitting his head."

Ebeth put her arms around Valencina to support her while she cried. She gently guided Valencina to a log where they could both sit.

Sometime later, Valencina took control of herself and Ebeth helped her wipe the tears from her face.

Valencina

"Come home with me and Rupert will do what needs to be done," Ebeth said, in a consoling voice.

"All right, Ebeth. You are such a friend," Valencina said.

"I've been near you since your birth."

"I've always known you and you were always close-by."

The sun was at its zenith when the two women crossed the dirt road to Ebeth's house. Ebeth saw Rupert in a field behind the house; she doubted Valencina had seen him. Ebeth settled Valencina in a chair and gave her a cup of tea. She excused herself and left out the back door to talk to Rupert, giving him the sad news and asking him to see to the burial. Ebeth returned, bought in a tray of bread and honey for their mid-day repast. Neither woman was inclined to talk, each deep in their own thoughts.

The next sun, Xennis was entombed in the family crypt, alongside Rosina. Valencina accompanied by Ebeth returned to Ebeth's home, to attempt return to their regular lives. Rupert had cleaned Valencina's house so she could return when ready.

Five suns later, Valencina returned to her home and began again to return to preparations for the oncoming exploratory trip. She'd asked Timus and Edecón to tell Lagunas and Daleninar to meet in three suns to discuss final preparations.

The morning arrived for their meeting. Lagunas reported first, "Our meat is dried and wrapped for carrying."

"Ours is ready and wrapped too," Edecón reported.

"Do we have enough arrows?" Valencina asked.

"Lagunas and I have made as many as we can carry," Daleninar reported.

"Edecón and I will finish making as many as we can carry in the next three suns," Timus promised.

"All right, it sounds as if we're almost ready. We will begin the trip in seven suns," Valencina said. "I'll meet again with the council to report our departure."

On the seventh day, the sun rose to a clear spring morning. Birds were chirping and the sky was a clear blue. Flowers bloomed in the meadows. A warm breeze from the south made the day ideal for beginning the exploration. All five young explorers gathered at Timus' and Edecón's house to finish loading necessary items in their packs and make final checks. Ebeth made certain they'd all broke their fast and had adequate provisions. Each explorer carried a backpack of provisions, water and personal items, a shoulder bag of arrows, a bow in one hand and a walking stick in other hand. Valencina led the group, Daleninar and Lagunas followed and Timus and Edecón brought up the rear. They took a northeastern path through the forest for the first day. As the sun was receding in the west, they stopped to build camp for the night.

"We'll stop in this pine grove for the night. The soft needle ground cover should make comfortable places for sleep," Valencina said.

"I am tired, I'll fall asleep as soon as I've had some food," Daleninar said.

"We'll construct a fire pit," Timus said, looking at Edecón.

Lagunas helped the others to shed their packs and bags so they could rest. Timus and Edecón scraped the needles down to the soil and dug enough soil away with stone tools to create a place for a fire then enclosed the fire ring with stones to prevent the fire from escaping. Lagunas and Daleninar gathered tinder and wood for the fire. In their search, they also found a spring from which they could get water for gruel in the morning and refill their water bags. Meanwhile, Valencina opened one of the packages of dried meat and two loaves of bread. They consumed their evening meal in high spirits, banked the fire and settled for the night of precious sleep. They spent little time in frivolous conversation as the group was tired, though excited about their journey.

Morning came as light found its way through the forest to awaken the explorers. Valencina rose first to awaken the fire and begin heating water for the gruel. The others awakened shortly after Valencina started the fire and all were ready to break their fast as soon as the gruel was ready. They ate, doused the fire and covered it with the dirt that had been scraped away last night. Everyone repositioned their packs and bags to begin another day's trek.

Three suns later, the group bid the forest farewell and viewed the endless prairie. The brightness of the sun, having been shaded for so many days, was hard for their eyes to adjust.

"We must follow a direct line to the East. We must be sure of our direction each day is based on the sun in the sky. It must be directly in front of us in the morning and directly behind us in the evening," Valencina said. "As your leader, I will make sure our direction is true."

"I will carry your bag of arrows, great leader," Daleninar said, half in jest.

"No need for that, great follower," Valencina said, laughing. Everyone enjoyed a few moments of laughter before they began their trek across the grassland. The grassland was soft on their feet, not as soft as the pine needles but there was an absence of stones and tree roots as had been on the forest path in the hardwoods.

Several days on the prairie where firewood was non-existent and water scarce, found the explorers eating dried meat and bread for every meal. Though it was tiresome, no one complained. Just when the water supply was running lowest, Valencina spotted a stream and trees growing along the bank. "Look, over there," she pointed, "see those trees, there's water there."

Valencina

They traipsed, in high expectation, to the trees and the stream. "It's early, but let's make camp here," Valencina said.

"Edecón and I will make some fishing poles out of those saplings. We brought some line and hooks. Maybe we can have fish for our evening meal," Timus said.

"That will be great," Valencina said.

"I'll look for tinder and wood for a fire," Daleninar volunteered.

"I'll prepare a place for the fire," Lagunas said.

"I'll fill the water skins for drinking and cooking," Valencina said.

Timus and Edecón brought three large bordallo for the evening meal. Lagunas and Daleninar had the fire ready for roasting, red coals with a light covering of ash. Three more saplings were chopped down to be used as grill poles across the fire. The fish were placed on the poles to cook while Valencina added a few wild onions for seasoning. As the sun was setting, the group enjoyed their meal of grilled fish.

"This is a good break from bread and dried meat," Timus remarked.

"I agree," Daleninar and Valencina said together. Edecón and Lagunas nodded with vigor; they couldn't talk because their mouths were full of fish. When they finished eating, Valencina banked the fire and the group spread their sleeping mats for a pleasant night of sleep.

Sometime in the night, Timus was awakened by a distant roll of thunder. *Our first storm*, he thought. *I better wake the other so we can put the sleeping mats away to keep them dry.*

Timus left his mat and proceeded to wake the others, first Valencina then Edecón, Daleninar and Lagunas. They reacted with haste, for having been sound asleep before the awakening. The thunder grew louder as they waited. Lightning flashed and the sounds of wind and rain were upon them within several minutes of their placing the sleeping mats under cover and retrieving their oiled capes that served as rain coats. They could do no more until the storm passed. The wind howled and a tree snapped close by. The group sat as close together as possible to shield from the beating rain and strong wind.

At last, the storm abated. The ground was too wet to lay out the mats for sleeping. Everyone was wide awake anyway. Timus thought building a fire was hopeless but Daleninar and Valencina dug under a pile of fallen tree limbs and chunks of wood and found some dry leaves and grass. The branches, though wet on the outside were dry beneath the bark so a fire was a reality. Daleninar put a vessel of water on the fire then added grains for gruel. As the sun was beginning to show itself on the eastern horizon, the group proceeded to break their fast. After everyone finished, Valencina said they would load their packs and begin the trek east.

Seven suns later, Valencina spotted a distant wall far ahead. Evening was upon them so she decided they'd make camp and proceed toward the wall in the morning. Rather than build a fire to alert whatever or whoever was behind the wall, Valencina directed everyone to eat dried meat, the last of the bread and drink water from the water skins, which was also running low. They finished eating and reclined on their sleeping mats for the night.

The next morning everyone was up at first light. They broke their fast with dried meat and water then packed and shouldered their bags to walk to and investigate the wall. By mid-morning, the wall was in front of them and walking around it seemed advisable, at least to Valencina.

"If we walk around the wall, we might be able to find an entry point," Valencina said. "Let's split up. Timus, Edecón and I will go to the left and Daleninar and Lagunas will go to the right. If one group finds an entry point, do not enter; wait for the entire group to assemble before contact with whoever is in this compound."

The group proceeded to do as Valencina directed. The sun was near its zenith when Valencina, Timus and Edecón stopped in front of a winding uphill path that looked to lead to a building. They waited a short distance from the opening of the path to wait for Daleninar and Lagunas. Soon Lagunas and Daleninar walked around the corner of the wall and joined the rest of the group. While they were discussing the path and to where it might lead, three men came down the path and saw the group.

"Are you planning to visit us?" the first man asked. He was a big man and seemed to speak with authority.

"Yes," Valencina said. "We are from a clan whose settlement is seventy suns west of here."

"You are a long way from home and have travelled a great distance," the man said.

"We are a group of explorers. We wanted to see if others are near and to learn from them," Valencina said. "We come in peace."

"Yes," the man said. "We can tell you are not a raiding party."

"I am named Valencina. I lead this group to meet the leader of a distant clan to learn something of their ways."

"I am the leader of this clan. I am named Canvol. Follow me into our settlement."

The group followed Canvol and his men up the winding path to the top of the plateau. They were in awe at the size and shape of the settlement. Houses built of what looked to be mud brick, streets with carts pulled by horses, people walking, children playing and, as they walked, a large building with a large smoke stack was visible.

As they approached an elongated, flat building, Canvol said, "This is where I work, where our council meets and all affairs of the clan are handled."

Canvol stepped aside, spoke to the other two men and returned to the group as the two men disappeared into the building.

Valencina

"Come with me so we can discuss our clan here," Canvol said, as he motioned them into a large room with several stone stools. "This is our council room. It is the only room for seats for all of us. Now, please tell me what you wish to learn."

"I am Valencina, the leader of this exploratory group. We come to learn what are your successes and if you wish to tell us, your disappointments. How have you built such an impressive settlement and why have you enclosed it in a wall? Do you fear a raid?"

"No, no, we do not fear a raid. We've not been raided since before I became clan chief. The wall was built to keep our livestock within the boundaries of the settlement at night. You see, the wall is for protection from wild animals. The gate is closed at night. Wild cats could still climb over the gate but we have watchmen to protect from that. We built the settlement over time as our clan grew and only built the wall a short time before I became chief."

"That is most interesting," Valencina said. "What kind of livestock do you have? We've never heard that term before."

"Our livestock consists of wild sheep we captured and kept so, over several generations, they've ceased to be wild. We also captured wild horses and performed the same with them as the sheep. We feed them, breed them and care for them so they have grown to depend on us."

"That is also interesting. We've never seen wild sheep or wild horses," Timus said, joining the conversation. "I'm Timus and a hunter. We are a small clan and our primary food is our kill of wild animals. We live near a forest so hunting is our main source of meat."

"Yes and we gather wild vegetables and fruits from the forest also," said Daleninar.

"It sounds then as if you are, for the most part, a forest clan," Canvol said.

"Yes, I guess you could say that," Valencina said. "We don't exactly live in the forest but we depend on it."

"We have an empty house in the settlement you may use for housing. We will show you the different parts of our settlement so you can begin to realize how we live and work," Canvol said.

Within seconds, one of the men who had been accompanying Canvol earlier came into the room and waited for Canvol to state directions.

Canvol looked up at the man standing to his side and said, "This is Lamas. He will show you to the vacant house you can use then he will be sure you have the supplies you need for living here."

"Thank you, Canvol. Greetings, Lamas. We look forward to our stay here and learning from and about your clan," Valencina said.

Canvol rose and left the group in Lamas' care. Lamas realized Valencina was the group leader so, looking at her, said, "Follow me and we will first settle you in your new home."

They followed Lamas almost to the other side of the settlement. There Lamas said, "This house is available for your stay. I will go to get supplies for your use. I'll return in a short time."

Valencina

Valencina thanked Lamas and bade the group to go inside.

"Valencina, this is a wonderful house," Daleninar said. "There are three rooms, one for us and one for the men. This larger room is for sitting and eating."

"Yes, Daleninar, this is well above adequate. I am surprised we have been welcomed and accommodated so well, being total strangers."

"I think it is because our leader is a woman," said Daleninar. "I think men are more likely to be considered devious and warlike."

"That may be, Daleninar. Let's not mention that to the men, though."

Everyone finished unpacking their backpacks. They laid out their sleeping mats and stood their packs of arrows in the corners, with their bows against the wall nearby. They realized those armaments were not necessary now.

Lamas returned with supplies, including flour, meat, grains, cheese, vegetables, fruits and milk.

"Thank you, Lamas" Valencina said. "This is enough for us for many suns."

"Please enjoy your visit. Tomorrow I will take you to see some of our works."

"That will be appreciated. We came to learn," Valencina said, as Lamas left.

"He seems to be a nice man but doesn't talk a lot," Daleninar observed.

"I think he's shy," Edecón said, "after all, we are strangers."

"Quite true," Valencina said, "I'm sure he will talk more when he shows us their works."

"I hope we find out where that milk comes from, it is sweet and thick. I've never had anything so good," Lagunas said.

"And the cheese. It is wonderful," Timus chimed in, with a mouthful.

"You are all testing the new supplies, huh?" Valencina asked, laughing.

"You should try some, Valencina," Edecón said.

"It will be time for the evening meal soon. I think we should have some of the meat cooked over a fire with some fruit, unless you're not hungry now, after snacking," Valencina said, teasing.

"Oh we're still hungry," Timus said. "We'll start the fire."

The men worked together to start the fire in the fire pit in the center of the room. Daleninar and Valencina prepared the meat for cooking over the fire and fruit to have afterward.

They ate the meat. Nobody was sure what it was, nothing similar to what any had ever had. Each had a small drink of the milk and all agreed it was sweet and 'soft' to drink.

"It coats the throat," Daleninar said.

"That's the description I was looking for," Lagunas said.

Valencina

Valencina suggested they bank the fire and go to their mats. The next sun promised to be busy and interesting.

Morning came, bright and clear. Valencina rose and raked the coals to start the fire blazing again. She filled a large cooking bowl with water and added grain to make gruel. The others arose soon after Valencina started working. Within a short time, they were breaking their fast. After the meal, they put the fire out and prepared to leave for the day's excursion.

Lamas arrived. He'd brought another man, who he introduced as Ramel.

"We'll show you the Livestock pens and the copper smelter. I will take two of you to the smelter and Ramel will take three to the pens. Then we'll switch. That should take most of the day," Lamas said.

"That sounds to be a fine way of it," Valencina said. "I'd like to see the smelter first. Who wants to join me?"

"I will," Timus spoke first.

"All right, Daleninar, Lagunas and Edecón will go to the pens," Valencina said.

Lamas said "Follow me. We're heading to that building with the smoke stack."

"We'll head for the pens. You'll be able to smell them before we get there," Ramel told Daleninar, Lagunas and Edecón, chuckling.

Lamas and his followers arrived at the smelter. It was a large open building space with a huge oven. "This building houses the cooking of the copper. The oven is called a kiln. We found heating the copper makes it easier to work with; pounding it into various shapes for holding things called pans; shapes for points for armaments, and decorations," Lamas said.

"It seems quite warm in here. How hot is that oven?" Valencina asked, not yet familiar enough with the term 'kiln' to feel comfortable using it.

"It is hotter than you'd use for making bread," Lamas said, smiling. "You see, the kiln keeps it at a steady temperature for melting copper over a period of many suns, perhaps seven to ten. It is a slow process."

"Where does the copper come from?" Timus asked.

"From the ground," Lamas said, trying not to chuckle. "We mine it and I will show you the mines next."

Ramel and his followers arrived at the pens. Sure enough, the pen odors were noticeable well before their arrival. "These are the animals we have kept from the wild so long, they think they belong here. They never have to search for food as they did in the wild so life is good for them," Ramel said. "These sheep have long hair and it can be shaved from them and used to make winter wear for the clan.

"Over here are the goats. We've only begun to gather them from the wild since Canvol became our chief, about thirty-six moons ago. We use them for meat, milk and make cheese from the milk."

Valencina

"I'd like to know more about the process of making cheese from milk," Daleninar said.

"We can show you that in a different time, but soon," Ramel said.

"I'm sure Valencina will want to see it, too," Daleninar said.

Back at the smelter, Lamas took them to another, smaller building behind the smelter building where the copper was hammered into objects. There was too much noise to hear the spoken word so they watched several pans being fashioned as well as heads for spears. After leaving the hammer building, Lamas asked, "Do you have any questions about what you saw in that building?"

"Not at this time," Valencina said. "Probably after we've all discussed it at our evening meal, there will be many questions for you at the next sun."

"That will be fine. Now let me show you the piles of copper we've mined. Of course, we'll show you the mines a little later, but soon, Lamas said.

Valencina and Timus followed Lamas to a large pile of what looked to be large chunks of rock and two smaller piles where workmen were scooping rock and adding to the piles. "These are the piles of copper, though they look like rocks," Lamas said. "In the smelter, the copper is melted from the rock. The rock is at the bottom of the kiln and must be shoveled out after each smelting process. It is hard work and many men are involved in the work. It must be done fast so the kiln doesn't cool completely."

"So it's hard and hot work," Valencina stated, as an observation rather than a question.

"Yes it is and the workers must be careful not to touch the edges of the kiln and the rocks or they would be burned," Lamas said.

"How is the kiln built?" Timus asked.

"As you've seen in your home, we construct our houses from mud bricks. We use the same kind of mud bricks to build the kiln. We add grasses and animal hair to the bricks to strengthen them, though the kiln bricks contain only small stones and mud because of the heat to which they will be exposed. The bricks won't last forever though, kilns need replacing every forty-eight moons or so," Lamas explained.

Ramel directed the three visitors to the area of horse pens. "These pens are larger to provide more area for the horses to move and receive food and water. They require large amounts of cut, dried grass and water. We also feed them grain," Ramel said.

"Why do you keep these animals that seem to need large amounts of feed and water? What is their purpose?" Edecón asked.

"They can be used to carry heavier burdens than a man can carry. Strapped to their backs, they can carry larger amounts of grass, pull heavier boxes of rocks and bricks for building and mining," Ramel said.

"It is now time to join the rest of the group and exchange places so you can visit the smelting operation and they can visit the animal pens," said Ramel. "In fact, they are coming now."

The group joined and a discussion started among them as Lamas and Ramel stepped aside to talk, for a brief time. In a few moments, Lamas turned to the group and said, "Let's change places and the new group of three will follow me to the smelter, while the group of two will join Ramel, to visit the animal pens." With that, the groups followed their leaders to find out more about the works of the clan.

The sun was low on the western horizon when the group returned to their house. "Let's build a fire and prepare the meat and some vegetables for our evening meal. Then we can discuss what we've seen and what we want to do next," Valencina said.

Meal preparations were accomplished, the fire roared then reduced to coals and the meat cooked. On purpose, Valencina had cut the meat into thinner strips so it would cook faster and be finished at the same time as the vegetables. Everyone was tired, hungry and wanted to discuss what they'd seen and where they wanted to go from here. After the meal, more wood was added to the fire and the group sat in a circle before the fire to discuss what they'd seen.

"I was in awe at the smelting process, I'm looking forward to visiting the mines tomorrow," Valencina said, beginning the discussion.

"I found the pens most interesting," Edecón said. "They use the horses to do the work of several men."

"The sheep have long hair and are shaved to use the hair for clothing and coverings," Lagunas said.

"I want to learn how they make cheese from the goat milk," Daleninar said.

"I'm interested to know more about the kilns," Timus said.

"We all seem to have developed interest in various aspects of this clan's works. If we are to learn the way these things work, we must try to become part of this clan and join them in as many aspects as we can," Valencina said.

"Do you think they'll let us work beside them?" Timus asked.

"Yes, I do. Remember, I told Canvol when we first arrived we wanted to know how they were able to grow so large and build such a wall. I think they'll let us work with them. This information is not secret. I think they're willing to share," Valencina said. "I will ask Lamas during our visit to the mine this next sun."

The sun was up and the group was ready to make more visits. Lamas said he'd take those interested in visiting the mines. Valencina and Timus stepped closer to him. Ramel asked those interested in the animals to join him. They all left for their designated visits.

Ramel found each of the three in his group were interested in different aspects of the animal pens. Because he realized he couldn't give adequate information about each interest at the same time, he said, "I'll find a cheese maker to help you find out more about cheese making,

Daleninar. I'll take you to the man who works closest and cares for the horses, Edecón. Then I'll work with Lagunas and answer your questions about the sheep, Lagunas."

Lamas was confronted with the same difference in interest in his group of two. "I'll first take you to the man who makes the bricks and builds the kilns, Timus. Then Valencina and I will visit the mines," Lamas said.

Valencia and Lamas walked a distance from the settlement to the mine but still within the wall. There Valencina saw men at work digging and lifting stones, horses dragging boxes on poles to make them slide across the sand to piles closer to the smelter. Lamas came back to Valencina. He said, "I'll take you closer to the mining work and into a tunnel if you want to see the work up closer."

"Yes," Valencina said. "I want to see it all. I want to see what copper looks like."

"Good," he said, "follow me."

As they arrived at the mine, Lamas explained, "Pits cover a distance of 4,431 cubits in length and nearly 590 cubits wide. The copper pits range from 148 to 433 cubits deep with connecting tunnels."

"I don't understand how you know the length of the mine," Valencina said. "What is a cubit?"

"We measure it using a form of measurement told us by visiting travelers from the south, many moons ago. It is useful to know how big something is or how far it is."

"Do you have to walk and measure it by hand?"

"At first, yes; then we get used to it or grow up with it so we know how far or long it is. If we need exact measurements, we have men who are trained in all our measures, not just length or distance."

"Can you teach me these measures?"

"Yes, of course. I'll show you at another time."

"Good. I'm anxious to learn new things."

"Now, let's walk through a section so you can see copper being broken from the ground and loaded into baskets."

They walked toward a miner striking a rock with a large stone hammer. *The sound is loud, nearly deafening,* Valencina thought. *The workers are strong men with well-developed arms and shoulders, probably from the work.*

"Are there any women working in the mine?" Valencina asked.

"No, women aren't strong enough to wield the stone hammers," Lamas said.

Valencina saw a hammer propped against a stone wall. "Let me try to lift that one," she said, pointing at the hammer against the stone.

"All right but it's going to be too heavy," Lamas said.

Valencina picked up the hammer and carried it to Lamas. "It is heavy but not unmanageable," she said. "Let me try to break that stone."

"All right but be careful."

Valencina

Valencina lifted the stone hammer over her head so to strike the stone in an arc as she saw the miner do. It was a perfect strike and bits of copper were visible. Lamas was looking at Valencina, with open-mouth. After he recovered, he said, "That was fine but to be a miner you'd have to do that from sun up to sun down."

"Yes, I'd like the chance to do that. I want to learn to mine so I can show my clan how to mine copper."

"Do you think you have copper nearby?"

"I'm not sure. I never heard of it until now. We will look for it."

"Here is a horse ready to pull the box of copper and stone," Lamas said.

They watched as the horse pulled the cart to the stone pile.

Daleninar learned to milk the goat after a few tries and the goat stopped kicking at this new, unskilled milker. She learned the soft, unforced squeeze of the teats in a rhythm that relaxed the goat as well as her. "Milking is actually fun," Daleninar said.

"It actually is," Monya said. "I've been doing it for many suns."

"Now, we'll take it into the cheese house and you will see how it is cared for and made into cheese."

While carrying the earthen vessel of milk, Daleninar followed Monya into the cheese house. "Now, we'll place the vessel in this tub of cold water to cool it for preparation for cheese."

"Why must it be cooled?" Daleninar asked.

"Milk must be cooled quickly so it doesn't sour," Monya said. "If it sours we can't use it. It would have to be thrown away, which is a terrible waste."

"Follow me to this table where the curds are removed from the animal stomachs in which it has been held for six or seven suns. These curds will be placed in earthen vessels, salted and are then ready for people to eat. Sheep milk is also used for this purpose."

"Are sheep milked in the same way as goats?"

"Yes, though it is a little harder because the sheep teats are smaller. Better to teach older children to milk sheep because their hands are smaller."

"I'd like to try that some time."

Yes, I'll get some sheep for you to try to milk in a few suns from now."

Timus was learning all he could about building a kiln and making bricks. "How do you build the kiln from the ground up?" Timus asked.

"A kiln is made up of two separated chambers, placed underground and one above the ground. An essential part of a kiln is a stokehole. It is a narrow strip formed as part of the underground chamber with which it is connected, though the length of the strip could vary. This is where the fuel is placed. The underground chamber, known as the firing chamber can differ in dimensions and shape. It had a relatively thick, perforated floor made of clay, called a firing floor, and a central pillar with arcs in a radial arrangement. The hot air circulates in this underground, tunnel-shaped space and, through the holes; the firing floor reaches the above-ground chamber, where the rocks are stacked with care. This chamber is covered with either a rounded or horizontal ceiling, which must be replaced more often than the rest of the kiln," said Zestus.

"Can you show me how you make the bricks for the kiln?"

"Yes, we're ready to begin making bricks within the next few suns. You can join me then. That way you can work with us on it."

"That is exactly what I want to do. I'll join you then."

Edecón received training in shaving the sheep. "We're just starting to shave a herd of sheep. Would you like to work with us?" Robar asked.

"Yes," Edecón said, with excitement, "I'm quite interested in these sheep."

Robar explained, "We use a sharp stone or bone knife for shaving. I prefer the bone knife. Now watch this man shackle the sheep in place with hide straps so it can't move. He's using a stone knife to begin to shave."

Edecón watched as the long gray hair fell to the hide on the ground under the sheep. The man worked fast and the shaving of both sides of the sheep was done in a short time. The man removed the hide from beneath the sheep, folded it and released the sheep.

"Now come with me to the inside of the building and see what happens to the hair," Robar said.

Edecón followed Robar into the low building. There were piles of gray hair being sorted by several women.

"The sheep hair is being sorted by the women for thickness and length," Robar explained. "It will then be washed by other women, dried and used for clothing. The hair that is judged to be too thick or thin will be set aside and sent to the brick makers to be included in bricks to build houses."

Lagunas spent his time learning about the horses. "The horses must be held for a time after capture," Damis said. "They are wild and must be tamed. We do that by feeding them, combing them, touching and talking to them. It takes about twelve moons to get them to trust us and allow us to begin preparing them for work."

"Are they dangerous when first captured?"

"Yes, they kick and rear up with their front legs. The hooves are strong and can kill a man if he isn't careful."

"Are these new, wild ones?"

"Yes, we've only had them for about two moons. Notice how they watch you. They don't trust you and would probably try to kick you if you went near."

Valencina

"I'd like to watch how a man approaches these horses to try to get their confidence."

"We can show you in the morning of the next sun how we approach them and their reactions."

"I'll be here. That will be interesting."

As the sun hung low in the west, the group all arrived at their house, tired, hungry, and ready to tell about their day. Timus, Edecón and Lagunas began the fire and Valencina and Daleninar prepared the meat and vegetables for the evening meal. The fire was appreciated because autumn was at a close and winter would be coming soon.

"It seems cooler here than at our settlement," Daleninar observed, after finishing the meal and sitting to talk.

"I think it is because we are on the plane here with no forest to the north for protection," Lagunas said.

"I agree, Lagunas," Valencina said. "The wind is coming from those snow covered mountains far to the north. There is no protection. It is probably cooler in the summer, though."

"Perhaps," Timus said. "We'll find out if we stay that long."

"I hope we do," Lagunas said. "I want to see the new horses become ready for work."

"Yes, and I want to be able to work with Zestus on a new kiln in maybe twelve suns," said Timus.

"There is much more to be learned in the mining and processing of copper. We've just begun," Valencina said.

Chapter 6

A New Home with a New Clan

The exploratory group decided where each of them wanted to concentrate first. Valencina opined they should explore at least three areas during their stay.

"Members must be able to take these work options home to teach the members of our clan. To be able to teach clan members who've never seen these activities in action means we have to be so well versed in these that we'll be able to show how they work. We may need to build a sample working model for clan members to understand, or at least be able to draw a picture of a kin, for example," Valencina said.

"That makes sense," Daleninar said. "I might explore sheep hair examination next."

"That is the idea. We don't have to decide right away but do give it some thought," Valencina said.

"Are you planning to work in the mines?" Lagunas asked.

"Yes, I do. I've tried using the stone hammer and, though heavy, I can manage. I need to know how to find copper, how to get it out of the ground, separate if from rock and how to make items from it. That means I'll have to work on at least three things and I may still want to try the animals," Valencina said.

"That sounds as if we're going to be here a long time," Edecón said.

"Yes, I told the council before we left we would be gone for twenty-four moons. It might even be longer. We have to make sure we can take back enough information to help our clan to depend on more than hunting," Valencina said.

"We will do our best, Valencina," Timus said. "I'm concentrating on the kiln and brick making now. I think I'll try mining next."

"We will all work hard while the sun is up and tell of our work to everyone after the evening meal at the end of each sun," Valencina said.

"I enjoy hearing about what others are doing and telling others what I am doing," Daleninar said.

"Yes and that is how we will make our experiences live in our heads and make us able to help our clan," Valencina said.

Valencina

Valencina lifted her hammer again, split a rock and the men working alongside her exclaimed, "That's a huge chunk of copper. Good work, woman." More of the men came to look at what she had opened.

"We'll be sure this gets up to the kiln on the next load. Who split the rock?" Kellner asked. Kellner supervised the miners and the loading of the baskets to be drug to the rock pile for the kiln.

"She did," one miner said, pointing at Valencina.

"A woman?" Kellner asked, in disbelief.

"Yes," Valencina said. "I've been hammering rocks for many suns now."

"I need help overseeing the basket loading and dragging rocks to the kiln," Kellner said. "Would you be interested?"

"If I'm needed there, I'll do that," Valencina said.

"Good, come with me. I'll show you what we need."

Timus found the brick making to be interesting, requiring exact measurement skills he learned quickly. He was left to make bricks with minimal direction and oversight. "Some of the best bricks I've seen made by a beginner," Zestus said.

"I enjoy the work. I feel an accomplishment," Timus said.

"We're going to make some changes on the kiln in a few suns. You can help and we'll use the bricks you've made."

"I'm ready as soon as you are to make improvements on the kiln."

Edecón entered the sheep pen and the sheep came to him. He had been feeding them and they anticipated another feeding. The sheep were comfortable with him. Robar noticed this and one morning spoke to Edecón. "Edecón, you seem to be getting on well with the sheep. They trust you. Springtime is coming on soon and there will be lambing. Can I count on you to help with the lambing?" Robar asked.

"Yes, I will work with you on lambing. Let me know when it is time," Edecón said.

"I'll show you some of the signs to watch for."

"That will be helpful. I'll watch."

Daleninar had made cheese with success and learned to add just the right amount of salt. Everyone who ordered cheese commented the cheese was better and the salt was consistent.

"We've received several complements from around the settlement. They're pleased with the cheese and, especially, the consistency of the salting. Please show me your salting method," Monya asked her, patting her on the shoulder.

"I'd be glad to show you. I have a copper cup that is just the right size for each bag of curds."

"All right, I'll start using it. It might be good for you to begin milking the goats and sheep."

"Oh, yes, I do want to learn to milk."

"Good. We'll start at sun up."

Lagunas had worked with the horses long enough so they came to him when he entered the large pen. He'd fed, brushed and watered them. Damis came to the pen one day, just as Lagunas had entered and readied to feed the horses. "Looks as if they know you and feel comfortable with you, Lagunas," Damis said.

"Yes, they are my companions now," Lagunas said.

"Good. The next sun, I want you to work with me getting them ready to pull the baskets from the mine to the kiln pile."

"Yes, I want to see how they work and how to get them to pull the baskets."

"It's not hard but you have to be gentle with them. Sometimes they are slow but it does no good to beat them. They can break their hitchings and run off. That would be a complete waste of all the time it took to tame them."

"I understand. I would not want to beat a horse, ever."

"Good man. See you next sun."

Talk at the next evening meal consisted of the compliments each had received and what their next work would involve. "We need to get more meat, vegetables and fruit. Also, Daleninar, can you get us more cheese?" Valencina asked.

"Oh, yes," Daleninar said, "Monya said I could have as much as we needed."

"That's wonderful. Be sure she knows how much we enjoy the cheese," Valencina said.

"Monya has heard it from many people. That's why she gave me so much credit," Daleninar said.

"We're all fond of it, Daleninar. I will be interested to know how our clan will receive it," Lagunas said.

"We'll have to have milk before I can make cheese," Daleninar said.

"That will be a problem," Valencina said.

The group remained quiet, each thinking about their life now and what they'd face, returning to their clan. *We're getting used to having all the things we don't have in our clan. How can I take these explorers back to our clan that has none of these things? I must think about it more and maybe talk to Canvol about it. I am their leader they and our clan expect me to bring back more and improve their lives,* Valencina thought.

Valencina began work at the rock loading for dragging to the kiln rock pile. "The baskets must be loaded according to size of rock," Kellner said. "Choose one large rock for the center of the basket and pile smaller ones around it and build what looks like a small mountain with a flat top. Three to four rows of rock is heavy enough depending on the size of the rocks. The horses are strong but they have their limits."

"That sounds reasonable. I'll begin by filling this basket," Valencina said.

Kellner walked away as Valencina set to work. After she finished, she called him to check the basket. "That will work well, Valencina. The horse should have no problems with that load."

Valencina had loaded several baskets when the first horse arrived. To her surprise, Damis arrived followed by Lagunas, leading the horse.

"All right, Lagunas, let's begin by hitching the horse to the basket. You wondered why we put a collar on him before we left the pen. The two long poles attached to the basket frame fit into the straps attached to the collar. Now it's ready to be pulled. Start him slow so he can get up momentum to reach the pile. When he gets going the sleds will glide easily on the sand over the harder ground," Kellner instructed.

Lagunas saw how simple the operation was. Valencina watched with satisfaction. I know now how this mining is being completed. *I'll work next on the kiln to complete the entire work from rock to copper items. I hope the others are able to complete their experiences as I have,* thought Valencina.

Timus and Zestus were at the top of the kiln, replacing bricks that had deteriorated because of the constant heat of the smelting process. Timus glanced down and saw Valencina loading baskets and Lagunas guiding the horse to the rock pile. He thought, *three of us are working on the smelting process, mine to kiln. How rewarding. We'll have a good discussion after the evening meal.*

Daleninar surprised Edecón when she appeared at the sheep and goat pens, milk vessel in hand. The vessel was deep and made of copper. It was bigger than the earthen vessel he'd used when learning to milk the goats. "Daleninar, you've arrived to milk the sheep?" Edecón asked.

"Yes, can you get a sheep ready for milking?"

"Yes, we'll put a ewe on the stand here. It holds her in place so you can milk her.

Daleninar began but could not get any milk.

"Let me show you," Edecón said.

He grasped her hands, which were holding the teats. He squeezed gently and the milk flowed. "All right, now you try it with that gentle squeeze," he said.

She did and it worked well. Daleninar was surprised. "All right, I've got it. I understand. It works the same as for goats," she commented.

"Yes it does. When you learn to milk, it works the same for any animal," Edecón said. "Of course, the size of the teats would make a difference, he added."

Daleninar completed milking and took her vessel back to Monya. "Wonderful. Did you have help or did you already know how to milk?" Monya asked.

"I met Edecón in the pens. He showed me how to put the ewe on the milking platform, tie her down, and get the proper squeeze to make the milk come out," Daleninar explained.

"Great. That means you are learning to work this together. That will help when you teach your clan when you return," Monya said.

Daleninar was a little surprised that Monya knew about their clan and they'd be returning to them. Yet, she realized they all probably knew the plan because Valencina had told Canvol about it in detail, when they'd arrived.

All members of the exploratory group continued to experience work into the next several moons. Life was quiet and they enjoyed their work. Then, one sun, everything began to change.

Chapter 7

The Raid

One morning after everyone had gone to their particular work, a loud "Wooooooo" sounded. Everyone stopped working. Valencina, Timus, Edecón, Lagunas and Daleninar looked askance at the clan members, with whom they were working. No one made a sound. Runners sent by Canvol brought the news; Lamas arrived first at the mines saying, "Raiders are coming. They'll be here soon. Everyone must come to the main square, now," He yelled, running on to the kiln and beyond. The people in the pens were given the same message by Ramel. Everyone dropped shovels, vessels and what they were working on and scurried to the center of the settlement. A crowd filled the square, men and older boys, as mothers and children knew not to leave their houses but to shelter there.

Canvol arrived and mounted a raised platform from which to address the crowd, "We will see the first raid in more than two generations. We have remained ready though. We have our wall and a strong gate against which we are stacking rocks. Our chief of armaments will distribute bows, arrows, spears and, if need be, copper bowls of molten liquid that will burn the raiders who it touches. The chief and his helpers will begin distributing armaments now."

Danual and his helpers proceeded to distribute armaments to the crowd. The explorer group left for their house to collect the bows and arrows they'd brought but did not expect to use, except for an occasional shot for some food.

"I'm glad we brought some armaments. They probably need all the ones they have," Daleninar said.

"They probably have enough for several suns maybe moons. I don't know what they've planned for; it has been a long time since they were attacked," Timus said.

"It's hard to know," Valencina said. "They seem to have scouts to keep a regular watch, so they know well what is coming and how soon. I'm amazed they keep a scout watch going in that it's been so long since they were last attacked."

Edecón, the one most interested in armaments, said, "A clan should never stop watching. We still have scouts, even though we haven't been attacked in most of our lifetimes. We have a good supply of armaments tucked under the council building."

"Have you been there and seen them," Lagunas asked in wonderment.

"Yes, I have. My father took me there once," Edecón said.

"Let's stop talking and get back to the square and find out what we need to do," Valencina said.

Everyone was craning their necks, looking north at a distant dust cloud being sent up by hundreds of striding feet. Sun shone off their armaments. "What makes their armaments, especially their shields, so shiny?" Daleninar asked.

"I don't know," Valencina said. "I'll ask Lamas. She elbowed through the crowd ahead to reach Lamas.

Returning a bit later, she said, "It's their new metal they call bronze."

"What is bronze?" they asked in unison.

"It is made from copper and another metal I've never heard of, tin," Valencina said.

"We'll have to learn more after this raid," Edecón said.

The horde was approaching. Lamas and Ramel were directing the defenders to climb the wall and use the floors of the circular parapets as had been practiced. *I've never seen them practice. I wonder when they do it. Probably when I've been too busy to notice,* thought Valencina. *I did notice some men leave their work in the middle of the sun; others took their place until the men returned and took up their work, as if they'd had a break. That may have been what the men who left were doing and the ones who took their place may have been practicing earlier or would later.*

The wall was populated by men with spears, bows and arrows. A large number stayed on the ground below to protect the gate from those who might climb over the stone wall protecting the main entrance. The raiders attacked, howling and shooting arrows that darkened the sky. Arrows dropped from the sky on those set to defend the gate. Many took shelter close to the wall, some fell, pierced by arrows. These arrows were unlike any seen by this clan. The arrows had bronze heads, harder and more damaging to bone and tissue than animal bone or copper arrows. The removal of such arrows was difficult and caused even more tissue or bone damage to the recipients.

The raiding horde could not scale the walls. The forest was far away but Valencina and the men on the parapet on which she was shooting saw a group break away and head toward the forest.

"They're going to get poles to make ladders to scale the wall," one man said.

"That won't take them long," another man said.

"How can they do that so quickly?" Valencina asked.

Valencina

"You've seen the ladders we use. They'll just cut the tall, new trees, cut smaller saplings and strap the foot holds to the poles; a quick job for those who know how to make them." the first man said.

"Why didn't they bring them, if they came from the mountains?" Valencina asked, between arrow shots.

"Too heavy to carry that far," a third man said, between closed jaws.

The fighting heated, getting heavier as time moved on. The sun was setting; there'd be no fighting after dark. Fires were being lit and tents were appearing on the grassy plane as the enemy raiders were preparing for the night.

Those who spent the day on the parapets were replaced by two fighters on each parapet for the night. These men had been held in reserve for the night watch. It was unlikely they'd try to scale the wall in the dark but it was necessary to keep watch with the enemy so close. Torches could be lit to help with a night raid if the raiders deemed it could be successful.

The raid continued for several more suns. Valencina maintained her fight on a parapet, a different one each day. This day was different though. The enemy brought the ladders to the wall. They had many ladders to place against several places on the wall. The enemy started up the ladders and the defenders shot the raiders as they climbed. It seemed easy at first but more climbed, one over the other so they could overwhelm the parapets.

This was the scene at the parapet from which Valencina was fighting. One raider poked his head over the parapet wall. In a circle, he slung something shiny connected to a strap. Valencina saw it and ducked but the man behind her did not and was hit in the face, nose broken, eyes and skull damaged beyond repair. Valencina bent down to assist but could do nothing.

"Call for help," she told another man on the parapet.

"I can't, more are coming up. We can't stop them," he yelled.

Valencina rose to look face to face with a raider. "Come on pretty woman," he said, grabbing her arm. "We'll take captives like you."

"No you won't" she said, wrenching her arm away and smashing his head with her other fist. Her arm strength had been honed by her moons in the mines. He was dead before he hit the parapet floor.

More came over the parapet but Valencina and the other two clan defenders were able to fend them off. Glancing down at the entrance gate, Valencina saw the enemy had scaled the stones protecting the gate and were flooding into the square below. It looked hopeless. Without time to see everything unfold, she did see Edecón and Danul directing more clan fighters to keep the women and children safe in their homes. When Valencina looked back, she felt a sudden pain, a sharp sting in her left hip. Looking down, she saw an arrow protruding from her hip. *Oh no, I've been hit. It hurts. My leg is so weak, I'm falling.* "Ahhhhhh,Owww," she yelled. It happened so fast she didn't have time to yell for help.

One of the men bent down to look at the arrow and her leg. "Our woman fighter is hurt, come up" he yelled over the side.

Some of those tending to the wounded were already on the wall. In a short time they came running carrying a stretcher of hide tied between two poles. Without attempting to examine or treat her, they grasped her feet and shoulders, placing her on the stretcher. Picking up the stretcher they hurried to the ramp to go below. Her hip was gushing blood by this time and they left a trail of blood all the way to a house that had been commandeered for treating victims of the fight. Along the way, Daleninar saw Valencina being carried to the victim house. She hurried to follow the stretcher bearers into the house.

"Valencina, what happened?" Daleninar asked, when Valencina was settled on a pad.

"I hurt too bad to talk much," she mumbled.

"You're bleeding. I hope they come soon," Daleninar said.

They came with water and bandages soon after. They told Daleninar to leave; the area was too crowded for visitors. Daleninar shrugged and went back to the battle. She heard screams from behind her that sounded to be Valencina. *They're probably cleaning the wound*, she thought, though she didn't know about the arrow in Valencina's hip.

After the battle each sundown, Daleninar brought a cup of willow bark tea to Valencina. Daleninar helped Valencina to drink, placing her arm under Valencina's shoulders and lifting her head a bit. At first, Valencina could barely swallow. She was close to unconsciousness from the pain. In time, Daleninar was able to get Valencina to drink the tea. Improvement began to be apparent and Daleninar thought they could bring Valencina home. Daleninar talked to Lagunas and Edecón when they arrived at the house. "Where is Timus," she asked.

"He was being carried off the far wall. I think he was injured or killed. I could not find out," Edecón said. "I'll go to the victim house to look for him."

"I've been there," Daleninar said. "I did not see him brought in."

"That's not good. I'll see what I can find out," Edecón said.

Through tears, Daleninar said, "Please let's not mention it to Valencina just yet. I want to bring her home so she can heal better and in full."

The battle had raged for twenty suns when the raiding clan gave up and left, never having been successful in overtaking the resident clan. Those still fighting left the wall and parapets to return to their homes and works.

Edecón found Timus had been killed and was buried in a mass grave with other clan members who'd been killed in the fight.

Valencina

Daleninar and Lagunas helped Valencina hobble to their house. When they arrived, Valencina had used all of her available strength. She lay down on the sleeping mat with help and promptly fell into a deep sleep.

"She'll want to know why Timus isn't here when she awakens. We'll have to tell her the truth. I'm not sure how she will react. She depends on him for many things, especially on the journey here," Daleninar said.

"We must be prepared to tell her as much as we know," Lagunas said.

"Which isn't much, I wasn't able to find out much. I was told he fell and never got up," Edecón said, voice cracking with emotion.

"All right, we'll tell her just that," Daleninar said. "I'm sure she'll have more questions, though."

"Won't matter, we don't know any more," Edecón said, fighting back tears.

"I'm sorry for your loss, Edecón," Daleninar said, as Lagunas and Daleninar went to check on Valencina.

"I'll go out for a while," Edecón said.

Lagunas said to Daleninar in a soft voice, "Edecón needs to grieve. He needs some time alone."

"Yes," Daleninar said, also in a soft voice, "we all need time to grieve for Timus."

Two suns later, Valencina was ready to settle in the general room and speak to Edecón, Daleninar and Lagunas.

"Tell me, where is Timus?" Valencina asked. "I thought he'd be back by now."

"Timus was killed on the wall and buried in a mass grave with other fallen clansmen," Edecón said.

"That is a huge loss," Valencina said, tears forming in her eyes.

"Did he d- d- die from an arrow?" Valencina asked, beginning to sob, as Daleninar reached for her.

"I'm not sure, Edecón said, "I saw him being carried off. I thought they were taking him to the victim house, but I understood he was already dead so they took him to the mass grave."

Valencina was overcome with grief as the others knew she would be at such devastating news. "Oh Timus, we all loved you so," Valencina sobbed.

Two suns later, Valencina said, "I will go to Canvol to find out how the clan survived and what, if any, work we can do," while they were breaking their fast.

"Yes, I heard they're going to keep the prisoners as slaves," Edecón said.

"I don't think they have slaves, Edecón," Valencina said.

"It's because they haven't been attacked in so long," Edecón argued.

"I need to talk to Lamas and Canvol anyway, so I'll find out what they're thinking," Valencina countered. "Everyone wait here until I return with a message as to what we should do."

Valencina

Valencina made her way, with a walking stick, to meet with Lamas and Canvol.

A gate guard summoned Lamas. When he arrived, he was shocked to see Valencina in a disheveled state and with a walking stick. "What happened to you? Why do you appear nearly in tears? I've never seen you look this way," Lamas said.

"Oh, Lamas, it is a bad time. We've lost Timus and I have a wound on my hip that is still quite painful," Valencina said. "I want to meet with Canvol."

"Please come in to the hall. I want to hear more," Lamas said.

Valencina hobbled with the walking stick and Lamas took her other arm as they made their way into the hall. "Sit here, Valencina; you've walked far enough. I'll have Canvol meet you here," Lamas said.

Lamas returned and said, "Canvol will be here in a short while. Can you wait here?"

"Yes, Lamas, I'm willing to wait for Canvol. He must be quite busy."

"Now what has made you so sad?"

"We've lost Timus. He has been most helpful to me and had a bright future with the clan."

"He was a good worker for us. He took a particular interest in the kiln and brick making."

"Yes, and he enjoyed the crafts part, making a variety of items from copper."

"He crafted an amazing torque for Canvol, too. He's wearing it right now."

"I didn't know he did that. Timus loved making things for others. He made this for me." Valencina held up her arm to show Lamas her wristband made of copper.

"Quite nice. A wonderful remembrance of Timus."

"Yes, I'll keep it forever."

"Now tell me about your wound," Lamas said.

Valencina related the entire event of being shot by a brass-headed arrow and her slow recovery.

"I am so sorry to hear of your being wounded. You must rest for now. Don't come to work until you feel ready."

"Your kindness is appreciated."

They sat in contemplative silence until Canvol approached them.

"I see you've spent some time with Lamas. He'll give me any news you've brought.

"Oh, Canvol, your torque is magnificent."

"Of course, you know who made it for me?"

"Yes, our dear, beloved Timus."

"You speak of him as if he is no more."

"Yes, Timus was killed in the last battle."

"That is a loss for all of us."

"We appreciate that, Canvol."

"What thoughts or questions do you have for me?"

"I came to ask what you plan to do with the fighters you captured," Valencina said.

Valencina

"It's simple. We'll put them to work in the mines for their meals and a house in which they will be confined," Canvol said.

"In other words, they'll be treated as slaves?"

"If that's what you want to call them. They may become clan members after a time, depending on their behavior."

"They may have much to offer. No one here knows how to make bronze."

"Yes, that's true. If they are willing to teach us, it will be to their credit."

"We must return to our clan before summer. I need to heal so I can lead my explorers to our home clan. I also want to continue to learn what Timus learned so I can teach my clan."

"We will help you as much as we can. Lamas is the one to call on if you need help."

"I appreciate your words, Canvol. I'll try to heal as fast as I can."

"Those things can't be rushed."

With that Canvol departed and Valencina began her trek back to her abode.

When she arrived at her house, Daleninar met her and helped her to a sitting place.

"Oh, Valencina, you had such a long walk. You must be exhausted," said Daleninar.

"Yes, it was far but I accomplished all I set out to do," Valencina said.

"The sun will set soon. Are you ready for the evening meal?"

"Will everyone be home for the meal?"

"Yes, Edecón and Lagunas will be home in a short while. By that time, I'll have the meal ready."

"Do you have some cheese for us?"

"Oh, yes, a new bag of salted curds."

Valencina watched as Daleninar prepared the fire, cooked slabs of meat and prepared wild onions and carrots for the meal. Valencina did not enjoy watching Daleninar work. *I feel so useless, watching my dear Daleninar do all the work to prepare the meal for us. I want to be able to get up and work too. I've never had to sit and watch other people work. My hip hurts as if the arrow is still there. It burns when I'm walking and aches when I'm sitting. There seems to be no relief. I don't want to complain, though. I have to be careful how my face looks too; Daleninar knows when I'm hurting. I don't know how but she seems to know.*

Edecón and Lagunas arrived to the house as the evening meal was ready. Everyone sat to eat. After the meal was consumed, Daleninar, Lagunas and Edecón wanted to hear about Valencina's day. Valencina provided all the details of her visit with Lamas and Canvol. She made the point to Edecón, "You were right, Edecón. Canvol is planning to use the captured fighters as slaves."

"Yes, and he would have done that to us too if we'd appeared to be raiders," Edecón said.

"Is that why you were concerned we might appear to be raiders? How did you know?"

"Timus and I heard it from our father. He told us what would happen if we were ever captured. He bade us not to tell others for fear of scaring the explorers."

"That was wise. Your father is a wise man. He should be the next clan leader."

"That is true but I don't think he wants to be clan leader."

"Few do, but someone must."

"I told Canvol, we'd be leaving before summer. He is prepared to see us off, I think," Valencina said.

"He's probably ready see the last of us," Lagunas said.

"Why do you say that, Lagunas?" Valencina asked.

"Damis and I have had differences about my leaving the horses. He thought I was going to stay forever, I guess," Lagunas said.

"Canvol set it up with Lamas and Ramel for us to change places every forty suns or so. Does he not remember that?" Valencina asked.

"I'm not sure. I think he just wants me to work the horses then he doesn't have to teach anyone else," Lagunas said.

"Maybe you're too good at what you do," Edecón said, joking.

"We don't want them to be dependent on us. That's why we're shifting around," Valencina said.

"I love working with the horses but I'd like to work on the kiln too," Lagunas said. "Would you talk to Damis with me?"

"I certainly will," Valencina said.

"Daleninar what will you be working on next?" Valencina asked.

"I want to work with the horses, if it is all right with Damis," Daleninar said.

"Perhaps you should come along with Lagunas and me when we go to talk to Damis. I'll tell him you are next to work with the horses," Valencina said. "I won't ask if it is all right with him, I'll just tell him that is the agreement." Valencina noted Edecón smiling when she finished.

"What's so humorous, Edecón?" Valencina asked.

"You're just going to tell Damis, not ask or tell him you planned it with Canvol," Edecón said.

"That's right. I'm just going to tell him. If he wants to discuss it with Canvol, he can," Valencina stated. "I won't hide behind Canvol. I made an agreement with him. He remembers."

By this time, the evening had advanced to night and all the explorers took to their sleeping mats.

As the sun rose, the group broke their fast and left for their work. Daleninar stayed a few minutes longer to make willow tea for Valencina.

"You haven't had any tea for a few suns. I think you need some to help with your pain," Daleninar said.

"You are right. Do I look as if I'm in pain?" Valencina asked.

"You are trying to hide it but I know," Daleninar said.

Valencina

"How do you know?"

"I watch people. I want to be a healer."

"That's wonderful, Daleninar. You must work with the healers when we get back to our clan."

"Can I work with healers here?"

"I don't know. I'll ask Lamas."

"Would you please? I'd love to learn more."

"I'm sure there is much to learn now, after the attack. Go back to your work now and I'll let you know what Lamas says."

Daleninar left with a lighter step, Valencina thought. *She's probably wanted to ask for a long while. I'm glad our conversation at last turned in that direction. She did show a good measure of compassion and desire to help during my time of pain. She seems to feel the pain herself. She will be fine working with people who are sick or in need of healing. I did not know of her interest in healing.*

Edecón came to the house first when the day was coming to a close.

"You are the first one home this sun; why so early?" Valencina asked.

"I learned something today that may explain why your wound from the arrow might still be so painful," Edecón said.

"Why is that?" Valencina asked, with interest.

"Danul said the enemy used poison on some of their arrow heads."

"That is interesting. It does seem slow to heal. Did he say what would help it?"

"No, if he knew, he didn't say. Should I ask him now?"

"No, Edecón, not right now. When Daleninar comes in, take her and you both can ask him."

"Why Daleninar?"

"She wants to be a healer and I think his answer and explanation would be good for her to hear."

"All right. Nothing wrong with that. I didn't know she wants to be a healer,"

"I didn't either until this morning."

Daleninar came in with Lagunas. She started to cook the evening meal as soon as she removed her outer wrap. Edecón and Lagunas prepared the fire. The meal was prepared in a short time. "Things are happening so fast this evening. Are you in a rush?" asked Valencina.

"Yes, Valencina, Canvol will address the clan at the center this evening. We want to hear him. We'll tell you about it because we didn't think you would be able walk there, stand in the crowd for the speech and walk back," Daleninar said.

"You are most right, Daleninar. It sounds to be something I'm not ready for, yet."

"That's right, Valencina. You will in time, but not this evening."

The group, all but Valencina hurried off to hear Canvol's speech. Valencina sat and watched the fire. *I wonder what he'll talk about. It's the first time he's talked to everybody since we've been here. Probably he wants to lift their spirits after the failed raid. Probably, he'll tell them, also, to be prepared for future raids. That's what I'd do, anyway.*

Valencina had dropped off to sleep, before the group came back.

"Shhh," Daleninar whispered to the others, "she is asleep,"

"Should we wake her and help her to her mat?" Lagunas asked, quietly.

""Yes, we better," whispered Daleninar.

Daleninar gently woke Valencina so she and Lagunas could help Valencina to the mats.

The next many suns saw Valencina improve at a slow pace, too slow for her liking. She visited Ramel and Damis so Lagunas could move on to the kiln and metal working. She made sure Edecón could split his time between horses and working with Danul in defense of the clan. Valencina went back to the mines, though standing was a problem at first, she persisted and gained strength in her hip to allow her to swing a stone hammer over her head while standing.

One day, she talked with a fellow miner, a slave. "What is your name?" Valencina asked.

"I am called Valanin," he said.

"Have you worked in the mine before? You seem to know how to swing a stone hammer at every rock."

"Yes, I have and my father before me and two older brothers."

"In copper mines?"

"Yes, but also in tin mines."

"I've not heard of tin mines. What are they like? Is tin in stone, as is copper?"

"Yes, tin and copper are sometimes together. It is not here, though. We have it in the northwest from here."

"Do you smelt it as we do copper?"

"Yes, that's the best way to get it out of the stone."

"So the mining is similar to what we're doing here?"

"Somewhat, but we have to remove topsoil to find the stone."

"That was done here too, long before I came."

"You've not always lived in this clan?"

"No, we're explorers from another clan, southwest of here."

"Why are you exploring? We do it by raiding."

Valencina gave him a description of why they were exploring and how much more time they would be here.

"You will be able to leave?"

"Yes, we are not prisoners, just visitors."

Valencina and Valanin conversed often in the ensuing suns. At the same time, they moved to the kiln where they operated the kiln and worked at brick making. Valanin helped Valencina climb the scaffolding to replace bricks on the kiln. From there they made bricks and worked at metal craft.

Chapter 8

Going Home

It was springtime and time for the explorers to return to their clan. "Will you accompany us to our clan if I can persuade Canvol to release you? I think you would be a valuable addition to our clan," Valencina said.

"I would welcome that. I never expected such an offer. Do you really think it is a possibility?" Valanin asked.

"Yes, I do. I'll try my best. I'll talk to him on the next sun and I'll give you the answer."

The next sun saw Valencina making her way to Canvol's hall. The gate guard recognized her and admitted her at once. She entered the compound and was met by Lamas. "Good day, Lamas. I've come to talk to Canvol because we're preparing to leave, to go back to our clan," Valencina said.

"I've gotten so used to seeing you; I forgot you will be leaving. I will see if I can get Canvol," Lamas said, as he sped down the hall.

Another reason we need to leave. Twenty-four moons is almost too long. They've become so used to us, they think we're part of them, Valencina thought.

Lamas approached saying, "Come with me to the hall. Canvol is finishing a council meeting and will talk to you in a few moments."

Valencina followed Lamas to the hall and stood aside as the council meeting members disbursed. When the room cleared, Canvol motioned Lamas into the room. Lamas introduced Valencina as she entered. Lamas was excused so only Valencina and Canvol could converse.

"What is the reason you seek me out this day?" Canvol asked, smiling.

"Canvol, it is time for us to end our exploratory visit. I request permission for our group to leave your settlement to return to our own," Valencina stated.

"Yes, Valencina, your group has performed well in all your work and in the defense of our clan."

"We learned more than we expected and will return to our clan to improve most aspects of our settlement."

Valencina

"I am pleased we could provide these skills. You didn't expect to participate in our defense against the raiders though, did you?"

"No, that was not in our heads but it was valuable even so."

"And your wound has healed well?"

"Yes, I can walk better now, but there is still some pain, though I can ignore it almost always."

"That is good. Our healers are well versed in caring for arrow wounds."

"But you haven't had any recent raids."

"No, but the information has been passed down from father to son."

Sensing she might be running out of time, Valencina asked, "Canvol, I have another request of you. I have worked with a prisoner named Valanin for many suns. He seems to have much mining and smelting experience. He would make a lasting contribution to our clan. Can we take him with us?"

"Oh, Valencina, that request could cause problems for me with the other prisoners."

"Yes, I understand. We could take him out into the grassland at night and leave just before dawn. No one would see us leaving and we'd be gone before the prisoners were allowed to go to work. Bring him away from the prisoner house for disciplinary reasons and you won't have to explain further."

"You're thinking as a clan leader. You are making my job easier."

"It is what I would do in a similar situation, if I were clan leader."

"You'd be a good leader, Valencina. Now I want to tell you about the gifts I'm planning to give your clan."

"Oh, Canvol. We don't expect anything. You've given us experience we would not have had any other way."

"That may be but I'm giving you twenty sheep, twelve goats and four horses. Also, I'm giving you all of the food and supplies you will need for the trip."

"Canvol, we express our deepest gratitude."

"I'm giving you the animals we've held the longest, which means they are the most docile and easiest to drive to your settlement. They will still require your group's overall guidance and attention. Keeping them from predators will depend on where you choose to camp. Keeping away from water sources at night and keeping a strong fire burning will be an immense help."

"That is wholesome advice, which I'll implement as we travel."

"I can think of nothing else to tell you. Take your experiences and use them wisely."

"That we will do."

Valencina stood, bowed deeply and departed the hall. *I have much to do to prepare to leave. I must first speak to Lagunas, Daleninar and Edecón about the drive required of us. Then I will inform Valanin about his leaving and that, out of necessity, he must spend at least part of the night, a distance outside the wall. Lamas will tell me where he is. We have to load the supplies Canvol generously gave us, on to the horses.*

Lagunas can see to that. Edecón can oversee the sheep and Daleninar the goats. Valanin and I will help as needed. It will be a long trip but an exciting one, Valencina thought.

Valencina arrived at their house, spent but still pumped. She awaited the arrival of the group. Group members arrived over a short period of time. Edecón and Lagunas started and tended the fire, while Daleninar and Valencina prepared the meat, vegetables, and set a loaf of bread on the stone to bake. The evening meal was ready and consumed a short time later.

After the meal, Valencina opened the subject of their leaving and her conversation with Canvol. Everyone sat in rapt attention until she finished. Then they all started to talk at once.

"Please, just one talk at a time. Daleninar what is your question?" Valencina said.

"I'm to herd the goats. Will they be easy to move forward? How will I keep them from wandering?" Daleninar asked.

Edecón answered her, "I learned to drive sheep from Robar. He said to keep a long stick in your hand and walk alongside to slightly behind them. It's not hard. They'll just keep going as you head them at the start. The flock sticks together. The same works for goats."

"Thanks, Edecón. That doesn't sound too hard," Daleninar said.

"I'll oversee the loading of the horses. Who will choose our supplies?" Lagunas asked.

"I will do that. Tell me before the end of the next sun what supplies you will need for the trip. Daleninar and I will go to the supply house and place our orders," Valencina said.

It was dark and the fire was reduced to coals by the time everyone sought their sleeping mats. Valencina banked the fire for morning then retired.

Three suns later, the group was prepared to leave. They left the main gate led by two armed guards. The guards took them over the grassy plain to an out cropping above a small stream. There they found Valanin and the guards left to return to their clan. Now the exploratory group and the animals were set to head southwest to their home clan.

Valencina planned to head more south than west. "I want to avoid the forest. I will not be safe for the sheep and goats. Also, they'd be hard to drive through the trees and underbrush," Valencina told the group, at their first stop.

"How far south should we go before turning west?" Valanin asked.

"I will look at the stars tonight then I'll know," Valencina said.

"Do you read the stars?" Valanin asked.

"Yes, I know their positions at this time then I'll know how to return to our clan," Valencina said. "I'll show you, if you want to join me tonight."

"Yes, I'll watch the stars with you. I'd like to learn more about the stars," Valanin said.

That night, after the evening meal and everyone, except Valencina and Valanin, took to their sleeping mats; Valencina and Valanin banked the fire and went out on the grassy plain to view the stars. The night was cloudless and the moon had set, the stars were bright. Valencina brought her walking stick, not because she needed it but she planned to point out stars with more accuracy with it, for Valanin's benefit. They sat on the grassy mat, watching the stars. Valanin moved closer to Valencina. "You are a beautiful woman," he said.

""You are handsome too," Valencina said.

"May I touch you," he asked, shyly.

"Yes, give me your hand," she said.

Their hands met, both feeling an instant connection. Hand holding led to moving closer and Valanin reached behind her to wrap his arm around her shoulders.

"It's so peaceful and quiet out here," Valencina said.

"It's a perfect night," Valanin agreed.

He reached for her chin to pull her face to him. Their lips met. They tumbled backwards and the rest is history.

In time, both sat up. "We'd better look at the stars before someone of the group gets up and notices our absence," Valencina said.

"Yes, we should," Valanin said.

Pointing upward with her walking stick, Valencina said, "That star is above our clan home."

"All right," Valanin said, "How do we know to turn west?"

"That is a little harder," Valencina said. "See the smaller star to the left of our home clan star?"

"Yes, but v it is so small."

"When it completely disappears then we turn west."

"Where does it go?"

"I'm not sure. Maybe it goes behind the bigger one."

"Or the bigger one eats the smaller one."

"I don't think so, if that would happen then the smaller one wouldn't be back the next night."

"That makes sense. You are such a smart woman," Valanin said.

"No, Valanin, I'm not smart. I just observe. Let's go back to our mats and I'll keep watch on the stars another night."

The group continued to trudge south for thirty suns before Valencina directed them to head west. There was much celebration among the group for now they knew they were, in reality, heading home. "We'll be home in about forty more suns," Valencina announced, during the evening meal.

"Did the star finally disappear?" Valanin asked, speaking softly to Valencina.

"Yes, it is finally gone," she said.

"I hope your clan will welcome me," Valanin said.

"They will because I'll make sure they do."

"I didn't know you had that much power in your clan."

"I don't. I'll make sure they hear right away about the knowledge and experience you bring."

"Oh, about the bronze?"

"Yes and the more valuable information about the possibility of raiders from the north. We need to begin work on defense. You saw how important the wall around that clan was."

"I see. I'll help as much as your clan wants."

"They will want it, you'll see."

The exploratory group was up early the next morning, ready to be off and head west. The walk across the grassland was easy on human feet as well as animal hooves. Valencina walked well early in the day but her hip became painful near sundown, she resorted to her walking stick as the sun began to sink. They tried to stop each night by a stream or watering hole for the animals as well as to refill their water skins. The group could tell they were getting closer to the clan settlement when the ground became rockier and the grass more sparse.

They stopped near a spring at sundown one night. They watered the beasts and ate their evening meal. Valencina called Lagunas to talk with her.

"Lagunas, our supplies have dwindled. We only need three horses now. Please take one and go ahead to the clan and let them know we'll arrive in two or three suns. You will be able to travel faster with one horse. Take enough supplies for you and move out before any of the others are awake," Valencina said.

"I'll ready the horse tonight and pick out the supplies then load the horse before sun up."

"Yes, that will work. I will tell the group where you've gone when they break their fast."

Shortly after dawn, Lagunas left the camp, leading the horse with a bundle on its back. The others in the group arose soon after and wondered where Lagunas was.

"When everyone is seated to break our fast, I'll tell you," Valencina said.

This quieted everyone so they prepared to eat. Daleninar thought she knew so she asked Valencina when they were making the gruel, "Lagunas has gone ahead, hasn't he?"

"Yes, he took a horse and will announce our homecoming," Valencina said, in a hushed tone.

"This is going to be the best homecoming ever," Daleninar said.

"Yes, I'm looking forward to it too."

"The gruel is ready," Daleninar announced.

Everyone sat to eat, expecting to hear were Lagunas was. Many were suspecting what Daleninar had guested. Valanin thought he knew but asked the question, "Where is Lagunas?"

Valencina stood to address the group. "We are about two suns from home. I sent Lagunas on ahead to announce our coming so they can be prepared because, most important, we'll need pens for the animals."

No one seemed surprised but all were happy with cheers, song and big smiles. Cheers of "We did it." We're coming home." "Two more suns." "Praise the Sun god," "Valencina, Valencina, Valencina."

Valencina held up her hand for quiet at the last cheer. "All right, let's get to work, pack up and head for home."

Chapter 9

Arriving Home

It was about near mid-day on the third sun, when they glimpsed the settlement in the distance. "I'm so excited, I want to run all the way home," Daleninar said.

"You'd be too exhausted to enjoy it if you ran from here," Valencina said.

"I know, I'm just excited."

"Yes, I am too. They will be surprised to see the animals."

"I hope Lagunas has had time to have them help him build pens," Daleninar said.

"Yes, I hope so too. They'd have had to get poles from the forest if there weren't enough in the settlement."

"I don't think there would be enough for three pens but the sheep and goats could be in one and another for the horses until they can get another one built," Daleninar said.

"Yes, I'm sure Lagunas will lead a good building crew," Valencina said.

They walked faster than on any part of the trip. They were at the main gate a short time after the sun passed its zenith. The animals needed extra guidance to climb the slope up to the gate. The gate keeper opened the gate and Valencina noticed a new wooden gate with the poles having been replaced by bigger logs. *I wonder if they used the poles for pens*, Valencina thought.

As the group and animals arrived in the settlement the cheering and welcoming horns were wonderful to the human ears but the animals spooked and fast became difficult for Daleninar, Lagunas, Edecón and Valanin to control. Valencina watched, with pride, as the rest of the group brought the animals under control and they were safe in their pens. As soon as the raucous welcome began to slow, Ebeth came to Valencina.

Ebeth hugged Valencina in welcome and saying in low, endearing voice, "Welcome home, Valencina. We've missed you so. Come home to my house."

"Oh, Ebeth I've missed you too. I'll come home with you as soon as I talk to my group," Valencina said.

Valencina managed to bring the group together for a short time, telling them she was going home with Ebeth and they should enjoy the home coming. Edecón had befriended Valanin during the trip back so they continued to hang together. Valencina was confident Edecón would bring him to home for the evening meal.

Ebeth and Valencina arrived at Ebeth's home as the sun was sinking. "I'm so glad you're back, Valencina," Ebeth said.

"Yes, Ebeth, I'm glad to be back. It was a long, long trip," Valencina said.

"Lagunas told us a little bit about what happened to you. We want to hear all about your trip. We have much to tell you too. We'll wait until Rupert gets here for the evening meal then you and Edecón can tell us everything,"

"I'm especially sorry for Timus' loss, Ebeth."

"Yes, that was the first thing Lagunas told us."

"I'm sorry but there was no way we could bring his body home,"

"Of course not, Valencina; we did not expect that. We grieve in our own way."

The evening meal was a spontaneous event. Rupert arrived home, they all finished eating and talking began in earnest. Valencina introduced Valanin then she and Edecón told them about their stay at the clan settlement. It was late night when the discussion finished, questions answered and plans for the next sun were agreed. Everyone went to their sleeping mats, exhausted.

Morning came and Rupert and Ebeth's household rose to break their fast.

Rupert said, "Valencina, please join me at the council meeting this morning. We have much to discuss."

"Yes, I must tell the council of our trip and what we've learned," Valencina said.

"It is best for you to inform the council as soon as possible," Rupert said.

"There will be a gathering on the settlement square later today where you and the rest of the group can meet with the settlement people and give them answers to their questions. I'm sure they are most interested in the animals you brought back," Ebeth said.

"It will be good but tiring. We must do it, though. We owe it to the council and the settlement people for their support. We need to begin to impart information we've gathered as soon as possible to help our clan, the purpose of our exploratory group trip," Valencina said.

"That is true. I'm sure the clan members will be interested in your experiences and what they can do to improve their lives," Ebeth said.

"They will hear it from us but whether or not they use it to improve their lives depends on how willing they are to change," Valencina said. "It will take time for many of the changes to be made and even longer for the effects to be realized."

"That is almost always true of changes," Rupert acknowledged. "Your statement indicates your ability to organize and lead."

The council members took their places at a long table made of two logs broken in half lengthwise. Others invited to speak took seats on a log bench along the wall of the council hall. Rupert started the meeting by introducing Valencina, Edecón, Lagunas, Daleninar and Valanin.

Valencina began her recitation by asking those in attendance to implore the Sun god to care for Timus, our departed exploratory group member. "We beg you, oh great Sun god, giver of all we have, to care for our brother, son and neighbor, Timus. We honor you this day and on into the future." Valencina, leader of the Sun god worship was followed with absolute attention in religious service.

Valencina took the rest of her time to relate to the council her experience in copper mining, smelting and metal work. She then talked of an even more unheard of metal, tin and bronze. At this point, she introduced Valanin. He explained tin mining, smelting, combining with copper to make bronze. Of course, there were many questions some showing a lack of understanding, others showing disbelief.

Valencina took control of the meeting again by saying, "We must beg your patience and give us time to show you in detail how this can be accomplished. It will be a slow process. First, Valanin will build a model to explain how the process works. We must explore to find sources of tin for mining. Then and only then can we make bronze."

Next, Lagunas explained the horses he brought back and their uses. He said "The horses can be used to carry loads and pull sleds or carts. They will be useful for mining operations, for carting or sliding loads of rock to the smelters and carrying loads of wood or dragging large animal carcasses from the forest."

Edecón explained the herd of sheep, their value in hair and milk, which caused the council to sit with open mouths. He told how the herd would grow to feed and provide the entire settlement with a new kind of clothing, food and other useful items.

Daleninar finished the presentation with her description of processing the hair into fabric, milking and cheese making. "Cheese is a new food item made from milk and salt. I will show the women of the settlement how to make this new food," Daleninar finished by making this statement.

Questions and answers took additional time but the meeting ended with Rupert asking the group to stay and talk to individual group member if they had any more questions. The woman council member who earlier had been ready to criticize Valencina's exploratory venture cornered Valencina again. "Your group seems to have brought back much information that may or may not help us. I'm not convinced. I think you've wasted much time and brought back someone who talks strangely and doesn't belong here. Maybe he's a spy," she said.

Valencina had heard enough of her criticism and said, "We have not wasted time. You will see the value of our trip over time. Most, especially the mining of tin will require more exploration. These changes will affect every clan member's life for the better but it will take time. Please be patient and attend meetings where we will continue to tell you of our progress."

"I don't know how much time you're asking for but it seems to be never ending."

"That may be, change is gradual and involves much work for everyone. It will not happen as fast as you want."

"I don't like change at all. What's wrong with our life right now?"

"There is nothing 'wrong with our life right now'. It could be better with these changes, though."

"I don't see how it can be better if it takes a long, long time."

"You will see changes over time and you'll be used to one as another comes on so slow you won't even recognize it."

"We'll see," she said, leaving in a huff.

She is going to be a problem all the way. I hope she doesn't have too many followers. She must have some or she wouldn't have been chosen to be on the council. I must speak to Rupert about her to see if he has any suggestions as to how to manage her negativity so she doesn't thwart our work in the future, thought Valencina.

Valencina walked home with Rupert. "I need to ask you about the woman council member. She seems quite negative when she speaks to me, in person. I don't know quite how to respond to her. Do you have any suggestions?" Valencina asked.

"She doesn't speak well of any new idea, no matter how important or small it is," Rupert said. "She is against almost everything we bring up, with certain if it's something new."

'She was against our exploration from the beginning and now she's against our changes we discussed today."

"Yes, that is to be expected from her. The rest of the council doesn't seem to be swayed by her negative arguments."

"I suppose there is some value in hearing both sides of a proposal."

"True, if she provided a valid argument. Hers is just 'no. it won't work' or 'no we can't do it', no reasons why. She doesn't think she has to explain further."

"That makes her contribution almost worthless."

"Yes, it does. The council has stopped listening to her. I think that's why she brings her negativity direct to you, not during the meeting."

"That may be right. Should I ignore her or continue to state my argument for change."

"Both would be appropriate as long as your patience holds out."

"I try not to ignore people, though she'd be hard to ignore. I'll continue the argument for change as long as I have to."

"You have the right approach to dealing with people. As you know, our previous clan and council leader has died. I have taken the position until a new leader is chosen. I want to bring you to the council as our new clan, council and religious leader. Will you consider this?"

"Oh, Rupert, I've never thought about being the clan leader. That is an honor I'm at a loss to envision. We do need to discuss it further before I make the decision. I'll do it if you think I can make a difference."

"Valencina, you could do it. You have already made a difference. Your hunting skills honed your already apparent leadership qualities. The exploration trip made your leadership recognizable to everyone in the clan."

"Rupert you are making me take a new look at myself and the skills at which other leaders also have hinted. They've said 'you sound like a clan leader' or 'you're thinking like a clan leader'."

"Oh, Valencina, that should have been enough to get you thinking about clan leadership," Rupert laughed.

"No, I didn't take the complement as serious as I should have; I guess," Valencina said.

Valencina, Ebeth and Rupert joined the festivities at the center square. People were gathered around Edecón, Lagunas and Daleninar. "It looks as if Edecón has started the fire and is in the process of preparing the sheep to cook over the fire," Ebeth said.

"Yes, he watched them prepare it during our clan visit," Valencina said.

"It will be a good change from our usual deer and boar meat," Ebeth said.

"Yes, it is quite different. I hope people like it. I like goat meat better. We'll have some of that next spring when we have more goats," Valencina said.

Valencina was overtaken by a number of clan people who wanted to ask about the animals. "How hard is it to take care of these animals?" the first man asked.

"They are not hard to care for as long as they're kept in the enclosure. They were taken from the wild so they have a tendency to roam if left outside the enclosure. They will fall prey to wild animals, such as wolves and big cats if left outside the enclosure, Valencina said.

"Are we then inviting such animals into our settlement by having these here?" he asked.

"No, our being here and surrounding the enclosure will keep them out. Edecón is training men to be watchmen for the enclosures. They will be able to keep any wild animals out of our midst," Valencina said.

"It sounds as if you have good control of the animals, here and the wild," he said, with a smile.

Smiling too, Valencina said, "We can control our animals and just keep the wild ones away."

Valencina

Before leaving, a woman said, "You have brought many things back from you visit. Did you only visit one clan?"

"Yes, we only planned to visit the first clan we came to. It happened they were interested in our staying to see all their works. There will be much more in the future. The animals are all you can see at this time," Valencina said.

"What is to come later?" the woman asked.

"Mining, smelting and metal works are in the future," Valencina said.

"That will be interesting to see. Your work is appreciated," the woman said.

"Your words are appreciated, too" Valencina said.

The day passed and, as the sun became lower in the west, the sheep meat was ready for serving. Edecón and Lagunas cut the meat with stone knives while Daleninar and Valanin formed serving lines to fill vessels people carried in their sacks or wound in their belts. As more people settled to eat, the talk decreased to near quiet, as the last were served.

There was singing and drinking after the meal. This was the cultural finish to a much needed celebration. The clan was together and needed to find something to be happy about after mourning the loss of their clan leader. The exploratory group had returned with the promise of something new. They'd experienced the first 'new' occurrence today and they liked it. The meat of the sheep was tasty and several clansmen wanted a hand in raising more sheep.

Valencina, Ebeth and Rupert arrived home too tired to visit further. They took to their sleeping mats soon after. Valencina experienced a vague awareness of Edecón's and Valanin's return but went back to sleep.

Four suns later, Rupert had arranged another council meeting and invited Valencina to attend. She had agreed after the celebration to be named clan leader. She did not know they planned to rename the position. Rupert stood and opened the meeting saying, "We are meeting today with the intent to name a new clan leader, but first we'll change the name of the position. In an informal discussion we decided on 'Chieftain' for the new title for the leader. Everyone who agrees, raise your hand."

Everyone but one, the woman council member raised their hands. Valencina thought, *I am not surprised she didn't want the change. She's the only one and she wants no change whatsoever. I'll not take it as a personal insult. She says no to everything.*

Rupert went on with his meeting, ignoring the no vote. All right, 'Chieftain' it is. Now I am proposing Valencina for the Chieftain position. I have discussed this with each of you, what say you?"

"Yes," was the overwhelming response.

Is there any one voting 'no'?

Valencina

The woman member raised her hand with some timidity but not unexpected.

"Valencina, please come forward and accept your position," Rupert said.

"I am honored and accept the position of Chieftain" Valencina said.

Rupert placed on her head the fur covered Helmut with red ochre stripes denoting her rank within the clan and the clan religion. She was now the esteemed leader in all clan endeavors, government and religious ceremonies, leader of all.

Rupert brought Valencina to the settlement square, where they stepped up on a dais to address the crowd who awaited the council decision. Rupert made the initial address.

"The council has chosen our new clan leader. Valencina, daughter of Xennis has been chosen…" much cheering, clapping and dancing ensued. When the crowed began to quiet, Rupert continued to outline her accomplishments, which many already knew. With that completed, Rupert took her hand, drawing her forward and stating, "I give you Valencina leader of the clan, Chieftain of all."

The crowd inundated her with flowers of all colors, shapes and sizes. She was almost knee-deep in flowers when they finished. Musical instruments of the day, string and pipe, were intoned and singing and dancing continued until the sun was setting.

The dais was cleared away and large tables were set up using rough-hewn planks and benches. Several women brought portions of the evening meal to the tables; people filled their plates and sat to enjoy the food.

When the evening meal was finished, the crowd moved to a large stack of wood and branches; they'd prepared a celebratory bonfire. It was a raucous affair, much intoxication, dancing and, of course, nudity and fornication. At this point Ebeth nudged Valencina and suggested they leave for home. Valencina, with gracious acceptance accompanied Ebeth home.

The next few suns saw Valencina drawing her government into shape. She selected Daleninar to be her second in command with many of the tasks of leadership open to her if Valencina became incapacitated. Daleninar would work close with Valencina, attend all meetings and advise when required. Valencina chose Edecón for all defense and building activities. Lagunas would be in charge of animal care, breeding and production. Valanin was named to locate and begin operations of the copper mine, later to lead an exploration for available tin. Valencina chose these clan members because she had worked with them in the exploratory group, knew their interests and capabilities and, most important, she trusted them beyond any doubt.

After the meeting, Valencina asked Daleninar to stay and speak with her further. "Daleninar," Valencina said, "I also need to ask you to select a group of interested women to teach how to make cheese and butter from the goat and sheep milk. They'll need to be taught to milk first, of course."

"Yes," Daleninar said. "Learning to milk is more difficult than making cheese, I think."

"If we can get cheese to be made in a particular place, they wouldn't all have to make their own," Valencina said.

"Yes, that's how the other settlement did it and it was most successful."

"Good. Let's work toward that. Teach the women to milk, hand the milk over to the cheese makers and they can get an amount of cheese based on the milk they deliver."

"Yes, they can keep some milk for household use and deliver the rest to the cheese house."

"That is the exact way I see it. Thank you, Daleninar. Now I must talk to everyone about their tasks. Would you please join me?" Valencina asked.

"Yes, my first task as your helper," joked Daleninar. The women laughed and went to find Edecón.

"Edecón, please take a few minutes and join us for a conversation about your tasks," Valencina said.

"I will. Let's sit under this big oak tree," Edecón said.

After all three were situated, Valencina began, "Edecón, you were given a large set of tasks today. I want us to build a wall similar to the one we saw at the clan we visited. Try to draw up a model in sand and mud to show us what you think we can build to satisfy our future defensive needs. Be sure to confer with Valanin because he was a member of the attacking force. Decide what else we should be doing for defense and let me know."

"Valencina, I looked at the wall and took some measurements. We can begin to layout the plan now. I think we also need to begin making a supply of armaments, including, spears, arrows and the burning pots, so effective in the other clan's defense."

"Those are good ideas. Be sure to involve Valanin when you need him. He is anxious to help," Valencina said.

"Yes I will do that," Edecón said.

"Thanks, Edecón," Valencina said as both women rose and left the tree.

Next, the two women sought Lagunas at the animal enclosures. "Lagunas, can you take a few minutes to talk about the animals/" Valencina said.

"Yes, Valencia," Lagunas said. "Let's sit on this rail bench."

"Lagunas, I need to know what your plans for the animals are."

"Well, Valencina, I plan to put them to pasture in an enclosed area, much the same as the pasture the clan we visited had."

"That is what I thought you should do. Edecón is going to build a sand and mud model of the wall. Be sure to work with him so he includes your pasture within the wall," Valencina said.

Valencina

"All right, I'll take some measurements of the pasture I'm intending to use then I'll talk to Edecón and see where he wants to go with that part of the plan."

"That will work well," Valencina said, as she and Daleninar turned to leave.

Now we must find Valanin to determine how he wants to explore and mine the copper," Valencina said.

"I think I saw him walking toward the stream after the meeting," Daleninar said.

"All right," Valencina said, "Let's head in that direction."

They found Valanin sitting on the streambank deep in thought. "Valanin, we've come to interrupt your thoughts," Valencina said.

"You did it quite well," Valanin said, laughing.

"I need to talk to you about the mining and exploration," Valencina said.

"Right now, I'm thinking about a plan for finding copper. Of course, we have to break open some of the rocks on the other side of the stream but, if they contain copper, we can begin mining here. It will be close to the settlement so workers will be easy to get," Valanin said.

"That sounds to be a plan that is workable and a good beginning. How soon will you be able to look across the stream for copper?"

"I'll get a group together and go at sun up. We should know by the end of the day, if there is copper there. I've been over there and the rocks look as if they may contain copper."

"All right, Valanin, as you know, all the rest of the plans for metal rests on a nearby supply of copper. Please do you best," Valencina said.

"We'll let you know what we find at the next sun," Valanin said.

The two women rose to go their separate ways, as the sun was well past its zenith.

Several suns later, Valencina opened a council meeting in the council hall. In addition to the five council members, Daleninar, Lagunas, Edecón and Valanin were asked by Valencina to attend. She intended to keep the clan council abreast of her intentions to fortify the settlement and develop industry for the benefit of the clan.

Valencina began by saying, "I have invited clan members who accompanied me on our exploratory travels to undertake planning for several aspects of change. Daleninar will begin by describing additions to our diet and clothing."

Daleninar stood, no longer the shy clan woman she'd been before the trip, "I came to tell you about the cheese and wool hair from the sheep. The cheese is made by pouring sheep and goat milk into stomachs saved from butchered animals. The left over contents of the stomachs cause the milk to curdle and age into a cheese-type consistency. The curds are removed from the stomachs and salt is worked into the curds. The salted curds are wrapped in hides and stored for 30 suns to age. The wrapped curds will then be available for women to pick up for their households. The wool hair has been stretched and is ready for spinning. We are building spinning equipment called distaffs and spindles. I will begin to show the women how to use these as soon as they are made. We're using wood and bone to see which works best or which ones the women prefer."

"Thank you for the report that tells us much of what you've learned from the trip and what you've brought back to enlighten our clan. Now, I'm asking Lagunas to tell us about the sheep, goats and horses he is overseeing," Valencina said.

Lagunas, a quiet sort, was no longer reserved, "I have taken the animal herds as my own. I have looked after them since we arrived home. We now have larger sheep and goat herds and one new horse. I am looking to find pasture for them. They are wild animals that have become dependent on us for food and water. Nonetheless, they are still wild animals and will roam again, if we do not enclose them. I am working with Edecón to solve this problem."

"Next, we'll hear from Edecón about his plans," Valencina said.

Edecón stood tall and seemed to fill the room before his booming voice demanded everyone's rapt attention, "I have come to tell you about a wall we plan to build to enclose the settlement and the surrounding mining and animal pasture activities. Our group witnessed first-hand the value of a wall for protection against invaders. Though we have not experienced invaders in my time, we have experienced attempted invasion in my father's time. We also need a wall to enclose a pasture for our animals as Lagunas just described. We seem to be moving forward and to continue, we need the help of all men, women, and children to work with us to complete these tasks."

"Now, we must hear from Valanin, as to where our mining effort stands," Valencina said.

Valanin stood, waited a discreet moment and said, "I have been charged to find copper, if it exists, close to our settlement. We found it does, just across the small stream below our settlement. We can begin by using the rocks above ground and, when those are used, we will begin to dig deeper in a circular fashion. The stone containing copper will be loaded on sleds that can be pulled by horses to the smelter. The smelter is yet to be built and that is under my direction with Lagunas' help. When the copper mine and smelter are in fine operation, I will lead a group north to find the nearest tin deposits. That exploration is still many moons away."

"Thank you, Valanin. That is an overview of what I intend for this clan. Some of you may feel overwhelmed or disagree with my intentions. I have seen all of these actions in a settlement no larger than our own. These actions fast become a way of life, what clan members begin to expect. We must make them a part of our lives. I insist these actions will improve our lives. Unfortunately, some of the council members and clan people who sent us on the exploratory trip are no longer with us or are unable to assist us to make the changes we've brought back. We owe these improvements to those who sent us to find new, better ways to live.

"Let us end with a prayer to the Sun god. Raising her arms high above her head and looking up, she began, "O god of the life-giving Sun, oversee and shine on our work to improve our lives. You give us food, water, earth and fire. Help us to help ourselves to have a safe and better life with these improvements. Inspire each and every clan member to work their best to fulfill our intentions." The council meeting ended with everyone still under the mist of devotion Valencina evoked with her prayer.

Chapter 10

Valencina Begins Her Rule in Ernest

The day began as most every day, except Valencina heard nothing from Ebeth or Rupert. She walked to their door and rapped softly, no answer. She rapped again, louder. Sill no answer. She opened the door and peeked in; both were lying on their mats, as if asleep. Valencina knew they were not asleep. She touched Ebeth, whose forehead was cold. She found Rupert just as cold. Both had departed this world during the night. Tears clouded her vision until she realized she needed to find Edecón and give him the news.

Where could Edecón be? Valencina wondered. *Maybe he's with Valanin or with*

Lagunas deciding on the enclosure. I have to find him where ever he is. It cannot wait.

Valencina left the house in a hurry, not noticing two men coming up the road below the house. She ran first to the pens but Lagunas was not there. She continued running to the stream where Valanin and a group of clansmen were breaking rocks. She ran across the steam asking, "Valanin, have you seen Edecón?"

"He was here but left to go to the forest to get sticks to begin his wall model. What is wrong?"

"It's terrible, Valanin. Rupert and Ebeth are both dead."

"Both are dead?"

"Yes, I must find a runner to get him home as soon as possible."

"I have one in our group who knows where Edecón went. I'll send him now."

"Oh, thank you, Valanin. When you have time, please come to the house to help Edecón."

"I'll give these workers direction and I'll be there soon."

Valencina said "Thank you" to the wind as she hurried back to the house.

Rupert and Ebeth were interred with family and many friends following the norms of sorrow and mourning. These norms considered death as a part of life and the departed loved ones' life or lives, in this case were celebrated. Rupert, having been a council member and interim clan leader, was celebrated by the entire clan. Council members and their wives planned and executed the celebration, including the meal, music and dancing, and a bonfire. Valencina enjoyed the celebration but her involvement in the joviality was tempered by the pain of her loss. Ebeth was as a second mother to her and Rupert had been her support as she rose in leadership, something of which Rupert had maintained and her father, Xennis, had dreamed.

Now, I must forge ahead, Valencina thought. *Alone...no not alone; I have Daleninar, Edecón, Lagunas and Valanin, the most loyal supporters I could ever have. Together we will give our clan direction and build a strong, self-sufficient, independent community. 'Where I go, they will go' is my goal of leadership. I must lead in a way that makes the clans people want to follow. It will not be an easy task. There will always be dissenters. I will deal with them, first by reason. If that doesn't make a difference, I will consult with my group supporters. I will make a formal statement, making them my advisors.*

I need to spend a little more time here before going home for some much needed sleep.

Several suns later, Valencina had formalized her group of advisors. She spent her time visiting the progress of the tasks ordained to move forward. Edecón had finished his model of the wall. It was designed to include the entire settlement, the pasture land for the animals the mining area across the stream and an area for the smelters, at least one smelter for copper, another for tin, and a third for combining copper and tin to make bronze.

"That is a well-designed wall model, Edecón. I see you will build parapets as they had on the wall we saw and stood on," Valencina said.

"Yes, Edecón said, "as we grow and develop, we will be seen by other tribes, most likely from the north. We'll need to build a strong defense as we develop our mining and metal works."

"That is my thought. Be sure to keep this model for the next council meeting. I will ask you to introduce and explain it then answer questions at the next council meeting."

"I will do that. Maybe others will have ideas we haven't thought of."

"That may be. We'll try to have a discussion instead of everyone agreeing or dissenting and we'll listen with care to their statements."

"I think that is the way to proceed."

Valencina's discussion with Valanin was similar. In a sheltered, sandy area outside the main square, Valanin had drawn a layout for the copper mine and the smelters within the proposed wall. He had conferred with Edecón so Valencina could see no problems with the design. Valencina also bade Valanin to prepare to discuss it in a future council meeting.

From there, Valencina discussed the pastures and enclosures for the animals with Lagunas. He, too, had talked with Edecón so he was in agreement with the wall and the pastures. She encouraged him to be prepared to join the discussion when Edecón presented the wall to the council.

Valencina and Daleninar discussed the milking and cheese making areas and what will be required for that operation.

"We'll need a place for the milking of the sheep and goats. The animal needs to be held in place with the head between two posts, one movable to allow the head to enter then the post must be moved and held firm to permit milking," Daleninar described.

"Yes, we saw the milking operation. How is the best way to show or describe it to the council?" Valencina asked.

"That will be difficult unless we can get Lagunas or Edecón to build a sample, something small, out of sticks to show how it would work."

"Good idea, Daleninar. Now, what do we need to have a working area for cheese-making?"

"We'll need a building close to the milking place for the milk to be transported for making cheese. Inside the building we need long tables on which to layout and fill the animal stomachs and an area to knead the salt into the curds. I think too, it would be good to dig a cellar beneath the building, accessed by a trap door to store the stomachs while they curdle and age the cheese."

"That is good information and good thinking. Please talk with Edecón and Lagunas to find out how to proceed with your ideas. They may also have some useful suggestions."

"Yes, Lagunas had the idea of a cellar because it would be cooler."

"All right. I think you're off to a good start. We'll bring it to a future council meeting."

During the next sun, Valencina received word the council woman, the habitual nay-sayer had died. Daleninar reported the news and Valencina directed her to attend the mourning ritual as Valencina's representative.

Several moons later, Valencina and Daleninar discussed the existence of the council.

"Daleninar, I don't know why the council is there, in actuality. They are not active nor helpful on day-to-day activities and decisions. They just agree with everything I do or say. Not one of them ever has a suggestion," Valencina said.

"I'm not sure, Valencina. It's almost as if they are afraid to differ with you in any way."

"That's interesting. I have been thinking the same thing. What can I do about it?"

"I'm not sure, maybe call for a new election of councilors?"

"I wonder if that would make a difference. Would the new council have the same feelings as these?"

"I don't know. Let's ask Edecón, Lagunas and Valanin if they've heard anything. Because they work closer with clan people, maybe they've overheard something."

"That's a good idea. I just think I need to do something but what, I don't know."

Two suns later, Valencina met with her advisors. "The reason I asked you all to meet together was to hear what I perceive as my problem with the council. They are not active nor helpful on day-to-day activities and decisions. They just agree with everything I do or say. Not one of them ever has a suggestion. Have you overheard any comments?"

No one spoke up and everyone seemed to be looking at the floor, except Daleninar.

"Does this silence mean you've heard something?" Daleninar asked. "If you have, do not mention names but please tell us what you've heard so we can begin to solve the problem."

"A-A-All r-r-ight," Valanin stuttered, reluctant to share the comments, "I heard a worker say to another worker that Valencina is trying to work us to death and the other worker agreed saying, 'she should come down here and work. I bet she's never worked in a mine'."

"Nothing such as that but I heard a worker say, 'why do we have to do what another clan is doing? We were doing all right the way we were'," Lagunas said.

"I'm wondering if we need to confront those workers. Give them the facts," Edecón said.

"I'm not sure confrontation is the right way to deal with this matter but we can't let it fester, it will grow to a full boil. Perhaps, you should deal with individual workers one-at-a-time.
Talk to them and find out what made them think this way and what would they suggest and why,"

said Valencina, thinking aloud. "Do this in a friendly, non-hostile way, putting the worker at ease. The worker must feel we are only interested in their thoughts and ideas, which, of course, we are."

"That could work," Valanin said. "I wanted to talk to the workers but I didn't want them to realize I'd overhead them."

"Can you start a conversation when they are among a small group with whom you are eating or drinking?" Daleninar asked.

"I could try that at the drinking hall some evening," Valanin said.

"That sounds to be a good idea, Daleninar. Lagunas and Edecón do you want to try Daleninar's suggestion?" Valencina asked.

Lagunas and Edecón nodded in the affirmative and Edecón added, "I will listen and watch those who come to work on the wall. I want people who are willing to learn to make bricks, lay them, and work hard and fast. I want them to understand this is not child's play."

"I approve of that approach, Edecón. Perhaps, we've taken on workers who don't understand or want to work. They should be watched. They may shirk their work, depending on other workers to do more than their share to compensate. That is a form of stealing and must be dealt with," Valencina said.

"I'm not sure how all this relates to our council problem that Valencina brought out at the start of the meeting," Daleninar said.

"My point in bringing up the comments was, maybe, just maybe, one or more of the council feels the same way and is reluctant to bring it forward," Valanin said.

"You have made a good point, Valanin. Let's try to have each of you, not Daleninar or me, talk to individual council members again in a relaxed atmosphere, such as the drinking hall, to find if there are feelings of discord with the way I'm leading the clan. Make sure you are not acting as though you are on a quest to get information for me. Make your tone and demeanor friendly and relaxed.

"Let's meet again in ten suns to see what you've found and we can work on solutions." The group returned to their separate work places.

Ten suns later, the advisory group met with Valencina and Daleninar. "What, if anything have you learned from your meetings with individual council members?" Valencina asked.

Edecón was the first to speak. "May I speak plainly?" he asked.

"Yes, of course," Valencina said.

"Remember the woman nay-sayer who was on the council before we left on the trip?" Edecón asked.

"Yes, I do. She'd be hard to forget," Valencina said. The group chuckled at the memory.

"Well, her thoughts live on. She died but her family agreed with her, we were wasting time and resources. In addition, and this is where the problem lies, the family has taken it upon themselves to talk to others and have drawn some to her way of thinking," Edecón related.

"That is interesting and troubling," Valencina said. She lapsed into a mode of self inspection, *"What have I done? How can I deal with this? I don't want these council men to know Edecón, Lagunas, and Valanin have reported their conversations back to me. I will have to listen to the other reports and ask for advice. Oh, how I wish Rupert was here. He'd know just what to do. Well, he's not here so I have to solve this my way.*

Valencina came back to the conversation as Lagunas was saying he'd heard nothing but support for Valencina. The two he'd talked to said they'd agreed with everything she'd set in motion so far and they were prepared to speak up if they disagreed.

"That is good to hear, Lagunas. What about you, Valanin. What have you heard?" Valencina asked.

"About the same as Edecón. Valencina wants us to be the same as another clan. She doesn't respect who we are. She doesn't respect our forbearers," Valanin said.

"Thank you all for this information. I'll have to think long and hard about these statements and develop an approach. We'll meet in another seven suns," Valencina said.

After the men had left, Valencina and Daleninar went to a smaller interior room and closed the door. They sat at a small table.

"I'm so surprised that nay-sayer's venom has taken on a life of its own," Valencina said.

"I didn't realize she could and would poison future generations with her vehemence." Daleninar agreed.

"Now, I have to figure out how to deal with it."

"I don't want to think of it this way, but it could put you in danger."

"Do you really think so?"

"Yes. Edecón and I were discussing last night the mysterious deaths of his parents. It occurred right after the celebration. Rupert was a vocal supporter of the exploratory trip. The food was brought in by many but the council men's wives served the food they had access to who received what plate. Easy for one of them to poison two plates and serve them to the designated people."

"That is amazing and makes some sense. I would never have thought this possible of our clan."

"Our clan consists of the most, good people but there can be a rotten fruit now and again."

"That is a good observation, Daleninar. From now on, I'll eat only food you prepare."

"I think that's a good place to start. We have to be careful of crowds, also. Bone knives can be deadly."

"You re scaring me, Daleninar, but you are right. I must think about my own security, as well as the clan's."

"I didn't mean to scare you but I think Edecón would say the same. Let's talk about it at the evening meal tonight."

"All right. I'm anxious to hear what Edecón thinks. He is much more tuned to security than I am."

The sun had set and the evening meal was ready. The hide doors were secured from the inside and were double thickness. Edecón, Daleninar, Valanin, and Valencina sat at a table in an inner room behind the kitchen, well away from the front door. It also served as a food storage room so the sound did not travel out of the room.

After everyone finished eating, Daleninar said, "Edecón, I told Valencina about our discussion about you parents' mysterious death. I warned her of possible threats to her life."

"I'm glad you opened the discussion, Daleninar. I thought about that today after the meeting and was about to bring it up tonight. Valencina, we don't want to alarm you and we can't keep you from going out and about in the settlement but we do want to discuss some security options. Do you remember how Canvol always had several men surrounding him when he met with any of us or a group of people?" Edecón said.

"Come to think of it, yes, I do remember," Valencina said.

"That was his personal security force. I've talked to Valanin and Lagunas and we think you need one and probably Daleninar, too," Edecón said. They heard a gasp from Daleninar.

"Yes, you too, dear Daleninar. I don't want our leader or my wife to be the victim of an attack," Edecón said.

"Daleninar, they know you are close to Valencina. They could use you to get to her," Valanin said.

"I never thought of that," Daleninar said, as she rubbed her arms that had broken out with goosebumps.

"We're not used to thinking of our own in these terms," Valencina said, in defense of Daleninar.

"None of us have," Edecón said. "We thought Canvol was too fearful. Maybe he had a right to be."

"All right, I suggest we begin searching for dependable men to form a security guard for Valencina and Daleninar," Edecón said.

Valanin agreed. "You and I should make a list of individuals who we think are dependable then talk to each and determine what their ideas of security are and who should be protected, before we state why we're doing this. All right, let's work on this after we get our crews working tomorrow morning."

"Fine, I'll find you at the wall," Valanin said.

All right, I'll be there and I'll be ready when you get there," Edecón said.

After this, the women cleared the table cleaned the dishes and everyone sought their sleeping mats.

Several suns later, Edecón and Valanin approached Valencina. "We have found six men and three women who are dependable to the core. Their loyalty is without doubt," Edecón said.

"Bring them in and I will speak with them, one at a time," Valencina said.

"That will be done. They are working now and will be asked to come forward, one at a time," Valanin said.

Over the next three suns, Valencina spoke with each clan member selected by Edecón and Valanin. She found all to be of faultless character and loyalty.

"I have found all nine to be without fault. I will trust my life and Daleninar's life with them," Valencina told Edecón and Valanin.

"We will continue to be vigilant for seeds of discontent among the clan," Valanin said.

"Discontent is to be expected, Valanin. It is threats of violence that troubles me most," Valencina said.

"That we will weed out before it becomes a problem," Edecón said.

"I thank you both and will continue to govern as I think best benefits the clan," Valencina said.

Chapter 11

Valencina's Reign Solidified

Valencina, now comfortable in her reign, visited the copper mine, the construction of the near-complete smelter, the animal pens and pasture, and the construction of the wall. She found the construction of the wall to be the slowest of the new projects.

"What can be done to hasten the construction of the wall, Edecón?" asked Valencina.

"We are working as fast as we can. The construction of bricks is the slowest part of the project because each must dry before use. That cannot be rushed," Edecón said.

"That I know, Edecón. We need more workers making bricks so more bricks are drying and will be available to the builders."

"We will make bricks in more locations where the wall is to be built so the bricks will be ready when we get to that part to build the wall."

"That should make building faster, Edecón. I'm glad you see a solution."

The smelter was finished and pressed into service. Workers extracted copper and stored it in bins for future use. Copper was malleable so it was pressed into sheets when extracted from the bins. Lagunas oversaw the beginning of the use of copper for the making of kettles, pans, buckets and other large vessels. Much more copper was extracted than could be put to immediate use.

Valencina met with Valanin to discuss the copper situation. "Valanin, we seem to have six bins of copper with more sheets being pounded every day. I think we are ready to begin the search for tin," Valencina said.

"I think you are quite right. I am prepared to lead a search party for tin this summer," Valanin said.

"Please decide who you will take on the expedition and make a list of what you will need. I also want to know your proposed trip plan."

"I already know where we will travel."

"Where do you plan to travel?"

"North."

"North? To hostile territory?"

"Not that far north. We will find tin just above the Guadalquivir River. It's as far south as tin can be found."

"I'm glad you are confident in its location."

"I've only heard aged explorers from our tribe discussing it. If it's there, we will find it."

"I believe you, Valanin. Let me know who will go and what you will need."

Two suns later, Valanin returned to Valencina. "I have found three clan members who will join in my exploratory venture for tin, Vasilis, Tomlin, and Tanus."

"What supplies will you need?"

"We will take a horse to carry the tents, cooking vessels, simple armaments and some food."

"Sounds as if you'll need two horses."

"The rest are busy at the mine."

"I'll see about that. Plan to take two horses."

Valanin nodded and left. Valencina walked to speak to Lagunas.

Finding Lagunas at the pens, Valencina said, "Lagunas, I need a moment of your time."

"Yes, my leader, what is your desire?" Lagunas asked.

"Lagunas, I've talked to Valanin about his exploratory team. I think he needs two horses. Can you make them available?"

"The horses are being used at the mine. It will slow the mining operation but, yes, two horses can be freed for Valanin's use."

"The mining operation can be slowed. We need the tin. Thank you, Lagunas."

Valencina made a hasty departure and Lagunas went back to work on the pens, shaking his head. Lagunas saw a change in Valencina's demeanor since becoming sole leader but he surmised that's the way a leader must be.

Four suns later, Valanin's tin exploratory group was ready to leave. Valencina made sure they were sent off with flutes and drums playing and a crowd cheering. Valanin lead the group of four with two horses loaded to capacity. Flags fluttered and the cheering crowd silenced only when the group was well out of sight. Valencina declared the rest of the day a holiday. Tables were placed in the open square where a feast was to take place along with entertainment and drinking. She announced the next feast would take place if and when the exploration was a success.

Valencina directed Daleninar to take control of the celebration. Daleninar began by enlisting several clan women to roast the venison, make the bread and use their gardens for the vegetables to be cooked. She walked to the cheese house to make sure there was enough cheese. "We must have bowls of cheese for the entire feast. There must be at least fifty bowls of cheese available. We can't run short," Daleninar said.

Valencina

"We will have it ready," the cheese maker said.

Next, Daleninar found the flute players and drummers. "We'll need you for entertainment this night," she said.

"We'll be happy to play for the feast and after," the drummer said.

From there, Daleninar stopped at the drink maker who was happy to accommodate the crowd.

Daleninar called together the artists who enjoyed making flags, signs, wall hangings and other decorations to provide banners and other decorations for the feast.

Everyone had a job to do to make the celebratory feast an event on short notice. They knew Valencina expected great things from this exploratory group. For them to underestimate her was foolhardy.

Time for the feast arrived. Tables were placed in the square, a dais was constructed for the table for Valencina, Daleninar, Edecón and Lagunas; each diner brought their own eating vessels and bowls. People formed a line for food and drink. Serving women placed food and drink on the table for Valencina and her close associates. As the last people in line were served and seated, Valencina rose to address the crowd.

"Welcome all. We are celebrating the sendoff of the tin exploratory group. We have found an abundance of copper, which we are putting to many uses. We want more than copper. We want to make bronze. To do that, we need tin.

Why do we want bronze, you ask. We want bronze because it is harder than copper. Harder means more durable; it has many uses and withstands repeated use. Bronze is also better for armaments than wood, bone or copper. My exploratory group saw this first-hand at the battle that took Timus' life. We must prepare, an invader is sure to come this far south in time, maybe a short time. Our clan deserves the best we can provide. I will do that. Please, enjoy yourselves tonight and prepare to return to work tomorrow."

As she took her seat, everyone stood cheering and pledging their loyalty to her. She raised her hand to silence them and return to their seats and their food. The feast went off well and Daleninar received accolades from Valencina.

"Daleninar, you have excelled at planning and executing this feast. You are my most loyal and trusted member of my enclave," said Valencina.

"I want only to serve you, my dearest leader," replied Daleninar.

After the crowd had eaten their fill, the music began in earnest. Tables were removed with haste, allowing for dancing to begin. Drink flowed and the noise escalated. Valencina motioned to Daleninar, she was prepared to leave. Edecón saw the motion and cleared walking space for all three to leave for their home. As they approached their house, they saw someone skulk away from the door into the dark. "Who was that?" Valencina whispered.

"I don't know. I'll hunt him down," Edecón said.

"Be careful," Daleninar said.

Valencina and Daleninar entered the house, lit torches and checked all the rooms. "Nothing seems to be disturbed or no one is hiding," Valencina said.

"I think we got here just in time," Daleninar said.

They heard loud curses, beatings and fighting in the back woods. "Edecón must have found that one who was going to enter," Valencina said.

"It sounds as if there's more than one. I hope Edecón will not be hurt," Daleninar said, in a worried voice.

"I hope so too. It sounds as if there were more than one."

The sound ceased. Soon, the hide was moved aside and Edecón limped in and fell to the floor.

"Oh, Edecón," Daleninar said, as she bent to discern his injuries.

"I've been beat to a pulp," Edecón muttered.

"I will secure the hides from inside and get some water to wash the cuts," Valencina said.

"He's passed out," Daleninar almost screamed.

"He is hurt bad. We'll clean him as best we can while he is unconscious because our ministrations will probably be painful," Valencina said.

They washed his visible lacerations on his scalp, face, arms and legs. "He will have to tell us more when he comes to. I'll put a cool cloth on his head," Daleninar said.

Sometime later, Edecón began to moan. "I think he's coming around," Valencina said.

Daleninar rushed into the room and to his side. "Edecón, can you hear me?" Daleninar begged.

"D-D-Daleninar, is that you?" Edecón asked.

"Yes, my dear Edecón. We've tried to help you," Daleninar said.

"I need all the help you can give me," Edecón said, in a weak voice.

"I want to get you off the floor and onto your sleeping mat," Daleninar said.

"I don't think I can get up," Edecón said.

"I'll get the mat and you can stay here for the night," Valencina said.

She brought the sleeping mat and laid it on the floor beside him. "Now, we have to get you onto the mat," Valencina said.

Daleninar helped Edecón to roll on his side, while Valencina pulled the mat under him as far as possible. Then Edecón rolled back, which made him a little more than halfway on the mat.

"Now, the hard work for us all," Valencina said. "Daleninar, move his legs farther onto the mat. Edecón, you'll have to help her."

That completed and after Edecón and Daleninar rested for a few moments, Valencina directed Daleninar to help Edecón roll as far onto the mat as possible. When that was accomplished,

Valencina straightened the edges of the mat and asked Edecón, "Can you spend the night here?"

"Yes, I will be fine now," Edecón said.

Daleninar said, "I'll stay right here tonight, too."

"All right. I'll see you both in the morning," Valencina said.

The next morning, at first light, Valencina rose and made her way to the front room. Daleninar was asleep close to Edecón on her sleeping mat. Edecón emitted a soft snore so Valencina knew he was sleeping rather than unconscious. She decided to prepare the morning meal without wakening either of the sleepers.

Valencina had just completed the morning meal preparation, when she heard a soft voice from outside the front door. She did not want to wake the sleepers in the room so she left the house through the back door and walked around the side of the house to meet whoever had asked admittance. As she saw her visitors, she felt tremendous relief. There stood Lagunas and his wife, Tikka.

"Lagunas and Tikka, I'm so glad to see you. We had a frightening situation last night. Come around to the back door, come inside and I'll explain," Valencina said. When they were in the kitchen, Valencina whispered to them, "Edecón was injured last night when we came home and a man was attempting to enter our home. He was sleeping; we'll look to see if he or Daleninar is awake." They peeked into the front room, where they found Daleninar awake and up,

Edecón was struggling to sit up. Lagunas walked to Edecón and gave him the boost to sit up.

"Oh my, what happened?" Tikka asked.

"It was, I thought, just the usual night time marauder. When we got home, we caught him trying to enter the house. He ran and I followed him into the woods. I was attacked by several evil, well-armed men. I fought as long and hard as I could. They left me to die. I came to enough to struggle back to the house. I got inside the door and could go no farther," Edecón explained.

"That is a terrible thing. Do you think they were trying to get to Valencina," Lagunas asked.

"Yes, that is exactly what I think," Edecón said, "and maybe Daleninar, too."

"We have to do something...but what?" Lagunas mused.

Every one sat in deep thought. *My life may be in danger from my own clan. I never imagined this to be possible. I can't believe it but my faithful friend was nearly killed last night, for me. What can I do?* Valencina thought, as tears came to her eyes.

Lagunas brought them back to the discussion, when he stated, "I suggest we have our security team armed and with Valencina at all times. We have nine members now; we can choose more if needed."

"That makes sense, Lagunas," Edecón said. "There should always be three or four guards with her and three or four here at the house, inside and out."

Valencina

"We have enough for that arrangement now," Daleninar said.

"Yes, we need to train them and put them to work, now," Lagunas said, emphasizing the word 'now'.

"I have an idea to secure our doors. I will take rough-hewn boards, stand them upright, support them with a cross piece to make a door. We'll use boar hide leather for hinges and a handle. We saw doors made that way at the clan we visited," Edecón said.

"That would be a great improvement," Lagunas said.

"I think you should put that type of doors on your house, too," Edecón said. "You are close enough to Valencina to be in some danger, too."

Tikka gasped and reached for Lagunas' hand.

"I didn't think of that. I was just concerned about Valencina and Daleninar," Lagunas said.

"Please, everyone, think about yourselves as well as me. There is a problem out there and we must eradicate it," Valencina said.

"When I'm able, I want to hunt that gang. I won't do it alone, though. I'll need to have our team involved. There were several in the woods last night, Edecón said.

"Dissent is to be expected; violence is not expected or accepted. If and when we find them, their punishment will be a public spectacle," Valencina said.

Everyone in the room knew Valencina had spoken. She had made a decision; to counter it would be useless, if any of them had had the mind to do so—which none did.

Valencina asked everyone to share the morning meal. "We have plenty for everyone. Please join us. Your being here will help Edecón recover," Valencina said.

Daleninar helped her put the table together, while Lagunas and Tikka continued to talk in low tones to Edecón. As soon as everything was ready, Valencina asked, "Edecón, do you feel it possible to come to the table?"

"Yes, with help, I can get to my feet. My head still hurts but some food should help," Edecón said.

Lagunas and Tikka helped Edecón to stand, get his balance and walk the short distance to the table. When all were seated in comfort, Valencina invoked the sun god for a blessing, "Shine on us, oh powerful sun god, help us through this difficult time and repair your faithful servant, Edecón, so he can continue to serve you and his clan."

Lagunas and Tikka bade the house of Valencina farewell. Lagunas assured Valencina and Edecón he would begin to talk with the chosen guard team. Lagunas told Tikka, "I'm going to speak to Oresis, one of the guards, who works at the animal pens. I want to get these guards trained and working as soon as possible."

"That is a good idea. I can talk to one of the woman guards, if you wish," Tikka said.

"Yes I have one in my animal crew, Denisica," Lagunas said.

Valencina

"Yes, I know her. I work with her in the cheese house."

'That will begin my quest to train the guard to help Valencina."

"The trained guard will put all our minds to rest."

"After we talk to each and I find the others at the mine, we'll get them all together for training. I'll talk with Edecón again to discern how he wants them trained."

"That is a wise approach, Lagunas."

Five suns later, Lagunas had contacted the men from the mine, Jaris, Tokin, Camus, Gorpik, and Aosis. The other two women were Raia and Vila from the vegetable gardens and the animal slaughter house. Lagunas now had the entire guard ready for training. As Edecón had demanded, Lagunas had the guard meet outside Edecón's house.

"Edecón will be out momentarily. He is recovering from the battle he waged in the forest over eight suns ago," Lagunas announced.

Lagunas had just finished talking when the hide door moved and Edecón emerged. He showed the signs of the assault, bandaged head, cuts and bruises on his face, arms and legs. He depended on the walking stick for balance and gait.

"I welcome you. Your station will be known as the Protective Guard, for which you have volunteered. Valencina, Daleninar, myself, Lagunas and Tikka are considered endangered. Valanin will be considered endangered on his return, also. We will begin training by showing you the results of the vicious attack I underwent when I, alone attempted to stop the intruder who we had surprised when returning home after the celebration. Valencina and her entire enclave could have been attacked, mutilated and even killed. We cannot have that; we can't and won't visualize that." With that statement, the volunteers broke into a loud cheer of loyalty and praise.

"We will divide the Protective Guard into two groups. A group of five will protect Valencina and Daleninar at all times during the day. They will move with them when they work in the hall of government or as they walk throughout the settlement. The second group of four will protect the Valencina's house and grounds, at night or as long as she is in residence there. We will continue to watch this guard arrangement and make changes as we become aware of the need.

"We will provide armaments to each guard member and test the skills of each during the next suns. If more training is needed, we will continue until all are deemed ready as guards."

Edecón was nearly exhausted by this time. Leaning heavier on the walking stick, he limped back to the house.

Lagunas closed the meeting, "Thank you for coming this morning. Return to your places of work now. You will return here for further training for the next three suns then you will be assigned full guard duty."

Valencina

Thirty suns later, the guard was in full operation. Valencina found it cumbersome and hard to be comfortable with them.

"I think the guard is needed but I don't enjoy moving about with so many when I go to visit the work sites," Valencina said to Daleninar, one day.

"Yes, it will take some getting used to but we must have them," Daleninar said.

"I know but we must find the violent dissenters and make a final show of power."

"I think Edecón will do that now he has recovered from his injuries."

"We'll probably keep some of the guard after the final disposition of the dissenters."

"Yes, Valencina, I'm sure Edecón will encourage you to keep them."

Edecón arrived at the hall of government, reporting to Valencina, "Lagunas and I have found the dissenters we find are the core of the problem."

"How certain are you they are the ones and only ones causing the problem?" Valencina asked.

"We heard their loud proclamation at the drinking hall. They were sitting at one table in the middle of the room. The leader, well into his cups, rose to address those in the hall, stating, 'we must end Valencina's reign. She is leading the clan in the wrong direction. Who will support me as the new leader?' Only the five sitting at his table stood and cheered. Others in the hall looked down at their drinks. Some said 'No', but were drowned out by those at the cheering table."

"Find them and bring them to me," Valencina said.

"We will bring them in chains," Edecón said.

Valencina questioned each culprit, one at a time, "You are accused of disloyalty, proclaiming I am unfit to rule. What have you to say in your defense?"

"I was drunk and did not know what I was saying," each said in their defense.

"That is no statement of defense. Try again," Valencina said to each defendant.

"I have nothing more to say," each said.

"I will make an example of you to show the settlement what happens when clan members try to destroy my rule," Valencina declared.

Her next directive was to Edecón, "Take them to the square, chain them to poles. I will pass sentence on them tomorrow when the sun reaches its zenith."

The next sun, at zenith, the square was crowded with clan members freed from their work to watch the power of Valencina.

"I will pass judgement on these clan members who have chosen to make public a challenge to my rule. Edecón, bring the log forward; each condemned man will lose his head. He has shown hostile disloyalty to the leader of this clan, religion and all we do. Off with their heads."

Valencina

Two guard members rolled the short log on to the center of the square. Edecón, sword in hand, dispatched each criminal brought to the log by a guard member. Punishment was swift and final.

"Take this to heart what you have seen this day. I will rule uncontested from now until my end," Valencina proclaimed.

The entire crowd took to their knees, proclaiming undying loyalty to Valencina

"Arise and go back to your work. This clan will move forward," Valencina stated.

The sun rose to a fresh glow, where the first flowers of spring were in full bloom. The wall had been completed, surrounding the settlement, the pasture and the copper mining activity. The sheep flock had grown to over 100 animals, the herd of goats had grown to over seventy-five and the herd of horses numbered nearly twenty. Valencina overlooked the vast settlement, the mine and the pastures with due pride. She stood on a parapet built for her exclusive viewing, As she overlooked her accomplishment, she thought, *So much has been done in a little over twenty seasons. I have my enclave and the Protection Guard to thank; without them, I would not have been able to achieve this. More than that, the clan has worked to make this settlement the success it has become. It mirrors the clan we visited so long ago. My intentions have come to be. Rupert, Ebeth, Timus, my parents and all who supported us on that exploration, though now gone, would be proud also. Thank you all for the faith you have in me.* With those thoughts realized, she left the parapet and returned to the hall of government.

The spring had passed and summer was upon them. "It is time for Valanin to return," Valencina said. "I hope he has been successful."

"We should send two scouts out to watch for him. He will probably come through the forest," Edecón said.

"That is a good idea, Edecón. We must plan a welcoming feast for his return, whether or not he is successful," Valencina said.

"I will begin planning the celebratory feast this day," Daleninar said.

"All right, Daleninar, you planned the last feast well, so do it again this time. We don't know for certain when it will be but get everyone thinking about it anyway."

"That is my plan. Much can be done. The hunters can go to, perhaps, kill a boar. Banners and all those preparations can be done now, too," Daleninar said.

"Yes, and we'll gather the wood for a bonfire," Lagunas said.

"Splendid and the cheese making can be stepped up, too," Valencina said.

Preparations for Valanin's return were set in motion; now for the arrival of the guest of honor. The scouts followed the trails in the forest as far as was practical to tread, for several suns.

After eight suns of watching, hunting, killing and dragging back a boar, and completing the preparations that could be done in advance of the celebration, Valanin and his exploratory band were sighted by the scouts. One scout returned, running to the settlement with the news of Valanin's approach. "He's here," shouted the scout, as he ran up the entry path to the settlement. "They are all fine and well."

"Let the feast begin," proclaimed Valencina, when she heard the scout.

Daleninar rushed into action, speeding to the various sites of preparation. "Start the roasting fires," she commanded the cooks. "Build the tables," she told the wood workers, "Hang the banners," she directed the artists. "Finish the cheese," she told the cheesemakers. Last, she called on the flutists and drummers to meet Valanin at the gate.

The musicians had just arrived at the gate and began playing when Valanin and his group walked up the path to the gate. Valanin was impressed with the welcoming but not surprised. He was met by two of the guards. "Take me to Valencina," Valanin said. "Be sure my group is given water and can sit to rest, while I am with Valencina."

One guard took Valanin to the hall of government, while the other guard saw to caring for the exploratory group.

"Valencina, Valanin is here to report to you," hailed the guard.

"Valanin, what news have you brought?" Valencina asked.

"Valencina, I have brought the best possible news. We have found what appears to be an unending supply of tin, north of the Guadalquivir River. I have samples in this bag."

He opened the bag and handed two rocks to Valencina. "They just look to be ordinary stones," she said.

"At first glance, yes. Notice the color and 's' type of swirl through the stone."

"Oh, yes, now I see it. I would not have noticed it, if you'd not pointed it out."

"These stones must be gathered and brought back to the smelter for processing then combined with copper to make bronze."

"What will we need to make this happen?" Valencina asked, for the first time, at a loss to visualize the magnitude of the discovery.

"We will need carts to be built to haul the stones. Horses will pull the carts. We will need clan workers to pick up rocks and, in time, mine for more stones, as we've done for copper. It will require a settlement at the tin mine to supply the workers with housing, food and supplies."

"We can begin work as soon as the carts are built and those who are skilled miners are recruited to the task. We must talk of this as soon as the feast is completed. Edecón, Lagunas and Daleninar must hear of this before the clan is told. Much needs to be discussed and many plans must be made before work begins, in earnest."

"I agree with you. We will meet to have these, probably, long discussions starting the next sun."

"That is my plan. Now we must attend the feast. Enjoy the baths then join us for roast boar," Valencina said.

Valencina

"This will be a feast to remember," Valanin said.

Valanin joined Valencina, Edecón, Daleninar, Lagunas and Tikka to walk to the feast. They took their seats on the dais, overlooking the assembled people in line for food. They were served by the head cook, himself, saying, "It is my honor to serve you all. Welcome back, Valanin. We have prepared the best the forest can give us. The sun has blessed Valencina in many ways." Bowing to Valencina, he made a swift departure to return to the roasting fire.

After everyone was seated and drinks were served, Valencina rose. The crowd knew she was ready to address them, so speaking died away. "You have joined us today to celebrate Valanin's safe return." The crowd stood and roared "Valanin, Valanin, Valanin..." many times over. Valencina raised a hand and the crowd fell silent and returned to their seats. "Please enjoy the bounty of the forest, our gardeners, cheesemakers and many generous wives. We will have music, entertainers and a bonfire after the feast. Enjoy yourselves." Valencina finished, took her seat and began to consume her food.

It was too loud to partake of conversation, *eating is best now, we'll get a full description of the exploration during the next sun. Valanin will have interesting tales to tell but we also must make decisions and plans. Tales are best told around a fire, after the decisions and plans are made. We'll stay at our house then; I'll tell Lagunas this evening before we leave here. I won't stay for the bonfire and the dancing. Edecón and Daleninar may not either. Valanin will want to but I think he's probably too tired. Lagunas and Tikka will probably stay. Much has happened, which we must impart to Valanin, too.*

I wonder if Valanin has his eyes on a woman. He's never mentioned anyone, but that is his nature. I'll never ask him; he'd be shocked and bewildered, if I did. It would be unfair if I did. He is a trusted and hard-working clan member. I am so glad he has received acceptance in the clan.

The meal was finishing, more drinks were available at the drinking house. People were moving away and walking to the field for dancing, where the music had started and, as night came, the bonfire would be lit soon. *I need to speak to Lagunas and Tikka,* Valencina thought.

"Lagunas, I need to speak to you a moment," Valencina said.

"Yes, what is your desire?" Lagunas asked.

"I'll be going back to the house in a few minutes. We plan to meet at my house in the3 morning of the next sun to discuss Valanin's exploration. Be sure to bring Tikka when you come."

"I will do that. I'm interested to hear of Valanin's adventure."

"Fine, I'll see you then."

Valencina

After a sharp nod, Lagunas took Tikkas hand and left the dais.

Edecón and Daleninar agreed to leave with Valencina.

"I tire since my recovery," Edecón said.

"That is understandable, Edecón. You've jumped right back to all of your work. It is good for you to rest."

"I wonder how long Valanin will stay," Daleninar wondered aloud.

"Not long, I suspect. I overheard him telling someone, he'd be able to visit in a few suns," Edecón said.

"He must be tired after all the walking," Daleninar said.

"I would think so," said Valencina.

They arrived at the front door of their house to be greeted by one of the guards.

"Thank you, Jaris, for your attention. The celebration is in high gear, music, dancing and drinking. The bonfire will be lit soon. You should see its light from here," Valencina said.

"One of the guards will bring your meals as soon as they can get away," Edecón said.

"Thank you, we're looking forward to it," Jaris said.

Before they opened the door and everyone got inside, Vila arrived with food for the guards.

Inside the house, Edecón lit torches and they each found their sleeping mats. Then Edecón extinguished the torches and sleep came to them all. No one heard Valanin arrive about an hour later. He walked to his room and fell asleep as soon as he took to his mat.

Early morning light woke the household. Valencina was the first to rise. She began first meal preparations. Daleninar joined her to complete the preparations. Edecón and Valanin entered the room and the meal began.

"Valanin, we'll begin our discussion as soon as Lagunas and Tikka arrive. I don't want to start the discussion before they arrive," Valencina said.

"Yes, I think it's best if we go through details just once," Valanin agreed.

"We're glad you all made it back safely, though," Daleninar said.

"Yes, and I think we can tell you about the challenge to Valencina's leadership," Edecón said.

"Oh my, what happened?" Valanin asked.

Edecón launched into a description of his encounter with the group, his injuries, their forming the Protective Guard, Valencina's decision to stem insurgency and the public beheading of the insurgents.

"I saw the guards. I thought they were new, now I know why they're there," Valanin said.

"I think that problem has been solved but we must keep the guards, as a reminder to the people, if for no other reason," Valencina said.

"You are right about the constant reminder. It can do no harm but, nonetheless, I'm sorry to hear of the problem," Valanin said.

Valencina

"It was difficult but not surprising. We have overcome that and there will be problems in the future, which we'll need to overcome, as well," Valencina said.

"Hopefully not from within," Valanin commented.

"That is to be hoped," Valencina agreed.

First meal dishes had just been removed, when Lagunas and Tikka arrived.

"We can start as soon as everyone is seated," Valencina said.

A large hide was unrolled on the floor. Everyone sat in a circle to begin their discussion.

"Let's begin by hearing Valanin describe his exploratory trip," Valencina said.

"The trip began last summer when we transversed north to a short distance beyond the Guadalquivir River. I had heard of these deposits when I was in my parent clan. We had no problems throughout our journey to the tin field. By the time we found the tin, the weather was starting to turn cold, with winds from the north and snow in the air. We spent more time than I expected huddled in blankets around a fire. Days when the sun shone and the winds abated, we searched and examined the rocks and stones for the existence of tin. We searched the surrounding area for many suns to determine the size of the deposits. We found enough to be confident we could mine and carry all the tin we could use for now and future generations. When the days lengthened and the winds warmed from the south, we began our return journey. Again, we had no problems and arrived as you met us at the gate."

"Thank you Valanin for a succinct description of your trip. Now we must decide what we need to do to acquire the tin and make bronze," Valencina said.

"It sounds as if we need to begin a permanent settlement at the tin deposit so that mining can be accomplished with efficiency," Edecón suggested.

"Yes, I think that would keep the supply of stones constant. We also need to set up a hauling plan. We'll need carts, horses and drivers," Valanin stated.

"How many suns will it take for a horse and cart to travel from the mine to the smelter here?" Edecón asked.

"The distance is long and the carts will need to take as smooth a route as possible, ford the river and continue to our settlement," posited Valanin.

"I suggest we spend these next four seasons making a path for the carts, building a fording place for the carts, building a second smelter and finding clan members willing to resettle at the mine," said Valencina.

"Those are all necessary activities to be undertaken before the mine can be started," Valanin said.

"Yes, our builders will be pressed into service for this project. They've finished building the wall," observed Edecón.

Valencina

"I won't know how many horses are needed until we figure out how many carts will be used," said Lagunas.

"I can ask the artists to draw a cart on leather to show the design," volunteered Daleninar.

"That will be fine, Daleninar. Lagunas and I will meet with the artists to give them an idea of how the cart is to be designed. We saw carts at the clan we visited. I think these carts should be modeled after the ones we saw," Edecón said.

"We should plan to have a steady flow of carts to the smelter and return at peak performance," Valencina said.

"That is what I see. It will take, perhaps, at least eight seasons to achieve that level of performance, I predict," said Valanin.

"All right, where should we begin?" asked Daleninar.

"Good question, Daleninar. I think we must plant flags at the site to announce our intention to settle and claim the use of the area. Then we need to ask clan members here to find those interested in settling there and working the mine. Here, I say we begin work on a second smelter. Edecón, you and Valanin should go to the tin site to plant the flags, taking stock of the path for the carts and where improvements must be made. Lagunas, I'm asking you to begin canvassing the people here to determine their interest. I will call a meeting of the clan to announce our plan within the next three suns," directed Valencina.

"Thank you, Valencina, for giving us direction as to setting this newfound project in motion. I will provide an announcement to be delivered by settlement criers," Daleninar said.

"Valanin, let's decide when to embark on a trip to visit the tin site and check the path along the way for cart travel," Edecón said.

"All right, the sooner the better. I am ready when you are," Valanin said.

"I can leave the next sun at first light. I'll meet with my workers today and be ready to leave," Edecón said.

"Everyone has something to do for this new undertaking. We'll continue to work toward setting up the tin mine. Now, go to your work sites and begin to prepare for the next. This meeting is now ended," Valencina said.

Chapter 12

The Tin Mine

The sun for the clan meeting arrived. Valencina stood on the dais, surrounded by her enclave and two guards. As she raised her hand, voices receded to silence. "I have important news for you. We have discovered a large area of tin. This means we will be able to make bronze. Bronze is stronger than copper and has more uses, however, the tin is several suns from here. We must develop a settlement at the field to mine the tin, similar to the way we mine copper. It will be brought here by horse and cart. We will have a fleet of carts and we will need drivers. We will build a new smelter here to extract the tin. The tin will be combined with the copper to make bronze.

Lagunas, Daleninar, Edecón and Valanin will circulate among you, asking for volunteers to work on this important project. Those who agree to make this new settlement home will choose the name for the settlement. I will choose the governor for the settlement and the project. That is all I have at this time. As we develop this plan, I'll keep you informed. Please consider volunteering for this project. Now, return to your work."

Voices began to yell, "I want to go", "Choose me", "Please take me" and many more until the ruckus required guards to quiet the crowd. When order was restored, Valencina and Daleninar returned to the hall of government. As they walked into the room reserved for Valencina, she commented to Daleninar, "I don't think we'll have any problem getting volunteers."

"You may be right, but they can't all go. We have to be specific as to what skills are needed. We can't deplete our skilled miners here."

"Of course, you are correct. Let's make a list of the skills we need and the number we can use in the beginning. After we've started, we'll see where we need to add workers. We don't know how many drivers we'll need. Lagunas can help with that."

"I also think we must wait for Edecón and Valanin to return. We'll need workers to build the path for the carts and the ford at the river. Those volunteers must come first."

Valencina

"Yes, you are correct. We'll wait for their return before we make an effort to seek volunteers."

"All right, I'll continue to begin to make the list. I'll get Hopel to remember the list. He has a memory bested by no other."

"Yes, Hopel is best for that. He isn't skilled at anything else but his memory is unmatched."

Twenty-five suns later, Valanin and Edecón arrived at the hall of government. "Valanin and Edecón welcome back; what news do you have for me?"

"We traveled without difficulty. We planted the flags, naming our clan as the place of our work and settlement. We found the path to be in need of some building," Valanin said."

"We found the path to be useful in many places but will need rebuilding where hills will cause problems for carts and horses. We'll make the line of travel as direct as possible. There is the possibility of building ramps for a ford at the river on the trail. This work must be done before we begin the mining and settlement. I will find workers to make a path suitable for carts. This could take four seasons," Edecón reported.

"You have given us valuable information. Please begin to enlist volunteers for the path work. There is no time to lose," Valencina said.

Edecón and Valanin set to work finding volunteers with the tools and brawn to embark on the work. When a force of 100 volunteers were assembled Edecón said, "We must be sure the path is passable for horse drawn carts with four wheels. It must be wide enough to allow carts to pass going to and from the mine site and the settlement."

"If we mine enough tin, we may build a smelter at the mine site then haul the tin to the settlement. That, though, is far in the future," Valanin told them. Thus the work on the path began. From there, the settlement would be built and the tin mine opened, with Valanin in charge.

Four seasons later, the path was built and Valanin and Edecón sought volunteers to take up residency and work at the mine. Edecón urged volunteers to begin building huts for new miners and their families. The settlement would be self-sufficient with some help from the main settlement. The distance, however, precluded regular and immediate help. Carts returning from the main settlement would be available to carry supplies not regularly available in the mining settlement.

Edecón met with Lagunas to decide if a herd of sheep and goats could be driven to the new settlement. "Lagunas, we're planning to take some animals to the mining settlement. How many can we send?" Edecón asked Lagunas.

"Perhaps as many as 100 sheep and fifty goats," Lagunas estimated.

"That would be too large a flock for one drive."

"Yes, maybe two drives would be better."

"We'll not send the animals until the miners and their families are settled."

Valencina

"How about pens and pasture?" Lagunas asked.

"Those plans will be made now that we know how many animals can be spared from our flocks."

"I'll work with you and Valanin to plan the pens and the pasture."

"That will work well. Come with me to the site so you can help with the plans."

"All right, I'll have one of my shepherds oversee our flocks while I'm gone."

Two suns later, Edecón and Lagunas traveled to the mining site, where they met Valanin.

Standing on a small knoll, Valanin pointed to open grassland and said, "This is where I visualized the pens and pastures to be."

"It is quite acceptable. I think the pens should be closest to the settlement and some kind of wall should enclose the pasture. A wall similar to the one surrounding our pasture at the settlement would reduce the likelihood of predators. I would think wolves are active here," Lagunas said.

"That is a good observation, Lagunas. Edecón, will it be possible to build such a wall?" Valanin asked.

"Yes, we can build such a wall. Let's take some measurements and I will return to the settlement and enlist our wall builders to plan and build the wall," Edecón said.

Within six seasons, the settlement was built; a wall enclosed the pasture, the settlement and the mine. Over fifty families volunteered to live at the new settlement. Over fifty miners volunteered to work at the mine while their families opted to stay in the original settlement, or some had no families. Valanin declared those miners would be given seven suns every moon to return to the settlement if they desired. This would be accomplished with twenty miners given this allowance at a time, so as not to shorthand the mining operation.

Eight seasons later, the settlement was completed, peopled, the animals were in pens and the mining operation was sending cartloads of tin ore to the original settlement. Men and children performed the mining and washing and pre-smelting activities performed before shipment by cart to the main settlement.

Less than four seasons had passed when Valanin met with Edecón to discuss the operation as it existed. "Edecón, we need two smelters here on this site. The process begins with washing the ore. The ore is ground then smelted in covered crucibles, into which workers blow air through reeds. Droplets of tin become encased in molten slag, which is ground out, rewashed and re-smelted in a labor-intensive process. The cart shipping process is too slow and fraught with difficulties. It isn't working," Valanin said.

"All right, we'll shift the processing to this site and we'll try to get more people to move here to work the rest of the process," Edecón said. "I'll tell Valencina. She is trying to keep track of what's happening here as well as everything at the original site."

"Very good, Edecón. I should have realized from the beginning this approach we had set up was faulty."

"That's how we learn. Try and if it doesn't work, we take another approach."

Edecón returned to the original settlement and approached Valencina. Edecón related to her what Valanin had told him at the mine.

"That makes sense to me; I could see the initial plan was not efficient. Valanin's new plan is sensible. Now you need to convince those who were trying to set up the process here, to move to the mining settlement," Valencina said.

"Yes, I don't think it will be a problem, most of them have friends already there," Edecón said.

"We can use the second smelter here for copper production."

"Yes, the metal workers still need copper items to cover with bronze."

"That will complete the process."

Six seasons later, the tin mining and smelting process was accomplished without hindrance. The residents of the mining settlement decided their settlement needed a name. An interesting suggestion became the most popular then became the name for the settlement, 'Valatin'. They made flags and produced hide sheets with 'Valatin' emblazed, using a heated utensil. These hides were used as door and window coverings.

This naming of the mining settlement caught the residents of the original settlement by surprise. Not to be outdone by the fledgling settlement, residents met at the square and, after various suggestions decided on Valentin. "We will approach Valencina with our decision. I think she will see we used her name as a pledge of fealty to her. She is our inspiration," the leader of the citizens' group said.

The group approached the hall of government. They were met by Daleninar, "What is your business here?" she asked.

"We wish to speak with Valencina. It is important to us," the leader said.

Daleninar departed and returned in moments, saying, "She will see you now. Follow me."

The group dutifully followed Daleninar to the inner sanctum of the hall of government. Daleninar opened the door and announced the group, "Valencina, a group of clan members to see you."

"You have come to me, what message do you bring?" Valencina asked, with no preliminary words of welcome, as she was wont to do.

"We have come to you to tell you the people of this clan have met and agreed to name this settlement, Valentin. We chose this name in response to the mining settlement's naming of Valatin," the group leader said.

"I see," she said. "You refuse to be outdone by the mining settlement. I understand that but there is to be no competition between settlements. Each depends on the other for goods, resources and government. I accept the naming of our settlement and I will make a formal declaration of the name 'Valentin' soon."

"We thank you for accepting our name of 'Valentin' for this settlement."

With that, the group exited the room as Daleninar opened the door.

The settlement names chosen and agreed upon, the clan members returned to work. Within thirty suns, prepared tin began arriving by the cartload to Valentin. The metal workers, more than 100 in number, set to work making bronze by heating tin and copper and mixing them. As the two metals melted, they combined to form liquid bronze. The workers then poured the liquid into clay molds to cool. It was used to make many bronze objects, such as vessels, swords, knives, axes and tools for mining. Bronze was sharpened and made into arrow heads and sharpened knife blades. *The possibilities are nearly endless*, Valencina thought, when she visited the metal shop.

Chapter 13

A Visitor from the South

The suns passed as the metal works produced enough tools to increase mining activity to match metal production. Everyone had all the sharp knives needed, hunters were more successful than before because of the bronze arrowheads and the beverage provided at the drinking hall was better, drinkers thought, and never ran low. The beverage was now made in bronze vats and held in Bronze casks.

A scout, whose area of purview was south of Valentin to the sea, ran to the gates begging to be admitted without delay. "I must report to Valencina now," the scout yelled.

The guard opened the gate and the scout ran up the path, without acknowledging the guard.

On arriving at the hall of government, the scout announced, "I have news for Valencina."

Daleninar opened the gate and the scout ran into the hall and, out of breath, addressed Valencina. "You will soon have a visitor from the south," the scout said.

"Take a moment to catch your breath then tell me about this visitor," Valencina said.

After the scout's breathing returned to near normal, Valencina offered him a vessel of water. The scout drank the water and she said, "Now, tell me about this visitor."

"A ship has landed on our shore and a group of men has debarked, dressed in peculiar headdress and robes. A man who speaks our language said the leader of the group is Al-Hued and he wishes to speak to our leader. I said I would tell her of your coming," the scout said.

"Who is this Al-Hued?"

"He is from North Africa."

"I wonder how he heard of us and what he wants."

"He gave no further information."

"Did they have armaments or did it appear to be a battle ship?"

"No, no armaments and they appeared not hostile."

Valencina

"Thank you for the forewarning. I will prepare for their arrival. You have performed well. Rest now and spend time with your family."

"Thank you, kind Valencina."

Valencina knew the visitors would arrive in less than two suns. She and Daleninar discussed the approaching visitors. Not knowing their mission, they decided to meet them here in the hall and discern what they wanted. There had never been such a meeting so neither woman had any idea how to greet them or how to respond to them.

"We must greet them with appropriate formality," Valencina said.

"Yes, I remember how Canvol greeted us. He showed a welcoming face but his voice had some reservation, as if unsure of our intent," Daleninar said.

"Quite true, now that you mention it, how perceptive of you. We'll welcome them, but be reserved as to what we share with them."

"They should be here in the next sun."

The next sun started as did most of the past suns. Valencina and Daleninar settled in the hall of Government for another day of listening to local squabbles and reports of progress about the cattle, the mines, and the metal works. Daleninar kept a close watch on the gate to learn of the visitor's approach. Soon after mid-day, she heard and saw a commotion and a group of five strange beasts approach with riders on top of these beasts. She hurried to Valencina. "They're here and they are riding strange looking beasts with humps and long necks," Daleninar announced.

"I'll come to the door to look," Valencina said, as she hurried behind Daleninar.

Being careful not to be seen but still able to see the entourage, Valencina said, "I've never seen the likes of those animals. Maybe we'll learn about them now. Let's go back and be ready for them."

They returned to the hall for visitors and waited. Soon, a guard came in search of Daleninar. "Our visitor has arrived and requests admission to the hall and Valencina," the guard said.

"Valencina awaits the visitors," Daleninar said, as she rose to accompany the guard to the outer door of the hall.

"Our guests are most welcome," Daleninar said.

One of the guests who spoke her language slowly, said, "We wish to meet Valencina."

"Valencina awaits. Please follow me," Daleninar said, as she turned and proceeded to walk to the hall for visitors.

When the visitors stood inside the hall, Valencina addressed them, "Please come forward and introduce yourselves. I am Valencina, Chieftain of Valentin. Welcome to Valentin."

A swarthy man with black hair and a close cropped beard to match stepped forward and said, "I am Shirac. I will translate your language to Al-Hued and our language to you."

Valencina

"Thank you, Shirac. That will be most helpful," Valencina said.

At that point, Shirac and another man dressed in opulent gold robes leaned to speak in their own tongue.

"Al-Hued introduces himself and wishes to know if your people can care for our animals, the camels," Shirac said.

"We have animal pens but have never cared for camels," Valencina said.

"That is all right," Shirac said. "Our people will care for them if you have suitable pens."

"Daleninar, please call on Lagunas to be sure we have adequate animal pens," Valencina directed.

Daleninar left to find Lagunas while Valencina introduced Edecón, her advisor, to continue the meeting.

"We are interested in your work here. May we be shown your work within these walls?" Shirac asked.

"First, we want to know more about you and why you came to this settlement," Valencina said.

This statement, of course, required more consultation between Shirac and Al Hued. After an extended time, the translator resumed conversation. "Al Hued says he has chosen your settlement because it was close to the landing point of our ship. We are interested in setting up trade relations if you have objects to trade and are interested in such an agreement. If you are not interested in this plan, we will save us both time and resources and we will move on," Shirac said.

It was Valencina's turn to discuss this option with Edecón. They conferred for several moments before turning to Shirac. "We are interested in discussing a trade agreement with you. We will show you our mining and metal working operations if a preliminary agreement can be agreed upon," Valencina said.

After a moment of discussion with Al Hued, Shirac said, "Al Hued is pleased to work out an advanced agreement with you. When will we begin?"

"We are pleased you agree to work with us. Let us start the talks early on the next sun. Edecón will show you to a place for your repose. We will meet here for further discussion," Valencina said.

Edecón bid the entourage to follow him. Daleninar met them as they were leaving; assuring them there was a pen available for the camels. Valencina waited for Daleninar to enter before requesting her presence. "Daleninar, please join me. We need to discuss this interesting visit," Valencina said.

"What are they about," Daleninar asked.

Valencina gave her a summary of her conversation with Al Hued through Shirac. "Now, what do you make of this?" Valencina asked.

"Well, I need to give it some thought but it sounds to be a good approach for us, if an agreement can be reached," Daleninar said, hedging a little.

"Let's discuss it over our evening meal tonight and have Lagunas join us," Valencina said.

"I think that's the best idea. That way, all factors can be discussed."

"All right. That we'll do. Please get the word to Lagunas so he and Tikka can join us."

Evening meal preparations were in high gear as Lagunas and Tikka arrived. Daleninar placed cups and tray-like plates on the table. When everything was ready, Daleninar called everyone to the table. The meal was sumptuous, including roast goat meat, fruits, cheese and bread. Edecón raised his cup, signifying a toast. When all cups were raised, he proposed a toast, "To a prosperous and long-lasting trade agreement with those from the south."

All signified acceptance by standing to take the first drink. That toast was designed to begin the discussion of the upcoming deliberations to design a preliminary agreement. Valencina began by thanking Edecón for opening the discussion. "I drew almost all of my advisors here this night to discuss what we should and should not include in a trade agreement. We have never drawn up such an agreement and I am not sure where to begin. Your advice is necessary," she said.

Talk of such agreements was not experienced by any so, in consequence, questions began, most of which Valencina could not answer. "What do they want from us?" "What can we show them?" "Will they attack us?" "How did they know we had anything to trade?"

"All right," Valencina said. "Yes, there are more questions than answers."

Edecón entered the conversation by saying, "We need to develop answers to these questions as best we can this night. As an advisor for armaments, I say, the visitors are not here to attack nor do they plan to attack; however, I say we should not show them our bronze arrowheads, axes or swords. Those we keep secret."

"Edecón, how much of the mining and metal works should we show them?" Valencina asked.

"I think we should show them the copper mines, the smelters and how we make bronze. Whether or not we show them the tin mines is up to Valanin," Edecón said.

"I would have liked to have Valanin here for this meeting," Valencina said.

"We should send a runner to Valatin to get him. He won't make it here for a few suns but he should be here before the final agreement is struck," Edecón said.

"Yes, please see to that. Start at first light in the next sun," Valencina said. "Now, what about an answer to another question, 'What do they want from us?'"

"I think they want to advance their knowledge of works, the same as when we went on the expedition," Daleninar said. "I am convinced of this because of their interest in our settlement, the mines and the animals."

Valencina

"Do you think they knew all of that just by approaching us?" Valencina asked.

"Yes, I think she is right," Lagunas said. "When we took the camels into the pens, Shirac asked questions about the animals and I answered him."

"They talk to each other in their language and we can't understand, so we don't know what they have observed," Valencina added.

The meal was long finished by the time the discussion drew to a close. Lagunas and Tikka said their goodbyes then Valencina and Daleninar cleaned the dishes and cups. When all was completed, the household took to their mats for much earned rest.

The sun began early for Valencina and Daleninar. They broke their fast with a small repast of bread and fruit. Valencina expected a visit from Al Hued and Shirac and she was not surprised when she found them waiting for her.

"Welcome on this fine sun," Valencina said.

"May we talk?" Shirac asked, with a brusque tone he had not exhibited a sun ago.

"Of course," Valencina said, in a matching brusque tone.

"We are interested in seeing and working with your miners and watching the metal workers. We've not been granted access to those works. Are we not welcome?"

"You are most welcome as we discussed last sun. Our workers must find tools and places for you to work in the mines. We don't want our production to be slowed. You will need to spend some time watching before you can begin."

"We have not come to watch but to get a feel for the work."

"That I know. If you want to learn you must first learn some of our language. You already have good knowledge of our language; you must teach your men so they can understand basic words spoken about the mine, its tools and orders given by the leader."

Shirac took several moments to discuss the conversation with Al Hued.

When Shirac was able to converse again, he said, "Al Hued is asking how we can learn a language in a short time."

"You don't have to learn the entire speaking language, just words used in the mining work," Valencina said, becoming frustrated. "Speak with Edecón to find what words are most needed for mining."

"We will do that." Shirac said.

"You will work at our direction," Valencina said.

Shirac and Al Hued left to find Edecón.

"I'm not sure what those men really want. I'm a bit concerned," Valencina said to Daleninar.

"I'm more suspicious than you are," Daleninar said.

"I'm hoping they'll seek Edecón, talk to him and we'll see what he thinks."

"Yes, Edecón is able to see into people's minds and know what they're thinking."

Edecón arrived at their home shortly before Valencina and Daleninar.

"Edecón, glad you are here. We must talk at the evening meal," Valencina said.

"Yes, if it's about Al Hued's visit, I think we should," Edecón said.

"That's exactly what it's about."

Valencina and Daleninar set to prepare the evening meal. Edecón sent a runner to get Lagunas so he could join the conversation.

"I've sent for Lagunas to join us for the conversation," Edecón said.

"Good, yes he should join us," Valencina said.

They consumed the evening meal in solitude, with each lost in their own thoughts.

As Valencina and Daleninar cleared the remains of the meal, Lagunas entered the house.

"Lagunas, have a seat. Our discussion will begin in a few moments," Edecón said.

Valencina and Daleninar arrived in the main room, settling for the discussion.

"Daleninar and I are concerned about the true intent of our visitors. What do you think about their intent? Are they being completely honest with us?"

"It's hard to say," Edecón said. "We're only speaking through an interpreter. Reading Al Hued's thoughts is most difficult. If he could 'speak his mind' to us, we'd get a better idea."

"Quite true," Valencina said. "Shirac seems friendly one moment and aloof the next. He seems less open and friendly after a conversation with Al Hued. It's as if he's being told to not appear to be so friendly."

"Could be," Edecón said, "maybe Al Hued is concerned with decorum, you being the clan chieftain and his being of some importance."

"Yes, 'of some importance' is a good way of putting it. I don't know exactly what his role is in his country," Valencina said.

"I'm supposed to teach these workers how to speak enough of our language to work in the mines," Edecón said.

"That is what they request," Valencina said.

"Do they have copper and tin where they're from?" Lagunas asked.

"We're not sure. They say they want to know about it. Why, I'm not sure. That's part of what the uncertainty is about," Valencina said.

"I propose we go ahead, teach them enough words to work in the copper mine. We send a runner to Valanin and ask him to come down here or tell the runner what he thinks or if he will let them work in the tin mine," Edecón said.

"Are they only interested in the metals?" Lagunas asked.

"It seems so," Valencina said. "They have a narrow interest in the metal works. How much should we show them?" Valencina asked.

"As much as we determine," Edecón said. "We must not show any armaments. We will not show them how we make the kilns. They'll see them and probably figure it out on their own.

We'll not show them how the bricks are made, containing straw or horse hair."

"Yes, let's keep the animal care out of it. I already have to care for their camels, which is causing extra work for us. It is also draining our feed supply," Lagunas said.

"We did not expect to take on care of guests for an extended period of time," Valencina said.

"What is their honest intent? We haven't stated even a conjecture?" asked Daleninar.

"It's because we don't have any notion as to their real intent. We'll cooperate as well as is prudent at this point," Edecón said.

"Good summary of our situation. We'll carry on with prudence and see if more information comes to light," Valencina said. "I'll be interested to hear Valanin's reaction.

"We should know in a few suns," Edecón said.

"All right. Let's meet again when we hear from Valanin," Valencina said.

Six suns later, a cart bearing Valanin and the runner appeared at the gate of Valentin. The gate opened and the cart wheeled direct to the hall of government.

"Welcome, Valanin," Daleninar said. "Valencina is awaiting your words."

Daleninar and Valanin entered the hall. "Valencina, Valanin is here," Daleninar announced.

"Welcome, Valanin," Valencina said, grasping his forearm in greeting. "We are interested in your words. Did the runner tell you what we asked of you?"

"Yes he did. I want to meet Al Hued and his interpreter, Shirac. Perhaps, I can get a better feeling about their intent," Valanin said.

"I'll send a helper to find Shirac and bring them here," Valencina said.

As they waited, Valencina and Valanin talked of arrival of Al Hued.

Shirac and Al Hued arrived, in due time, at the hall of government. "We are here at your bidding," Shirac said.

Valencina introduced Valanin to Shirac. "We are here to learn about your mining and metal works," Shirac said.

"That is interesting. How did you hear of us?" Valanin asked.

"We have heard of the wondrous new metal, bronze, people from this land are making," Shirac said.

"It is quite new to us and we are still learning about making it," Valanin said.

"That might be why I detect a hesitancy of the people here to share information," Shirac said.

"I don't think Valencina and the people here are hesitant to share information. Because we are still in the learning and experimenting stage, we are not sure what information would be correct and final to share," Valanin said.

"That puts our mind to rest on that concern, if you speak for Valencina," Shirac said.

"Valanin speaks correctly," Valencina said. "Perhaps, it would be better for you to move to the north of our land, where bronze is in constant use and the people are better set up to give you the information you seek."

Shirac took several moments to confer with Al Hued.

"We cannot go further with our camels. We will go back to our homeland when we finish here," Shirac said.

"That is an unfortunate decision," Valanin said. "You could learn better from the northern people."

After Shirac and Al Hued left, Valanin asked Valencina, "Did you notice how Al Hued was looking you over as Shirac talked to you?"

"No, I did not. I was concentrating on what Shirac was saying," Valencina said.

"I hope I am mistaken but he had a lecherous look on his face as he watched you move and stand listening to Shirac."

"I hope you are wrong. I have no interest in any man, certainly not Al Hued."

"I think you make that clear but Al Hued may not be so quick to be put off, instead you are more enticing."

"I'm not trying to be enticing. I don't want to entice Al Hued. I just want him to leave."

"Yes, I understand. From now on, make sure he and Shirac only deal with Edecón. Make sure you are not seen about until they are ready to leave."

"That makes me a prisoner in my own settlement."

"Yes, in a way it does, but your safety and well-being is at stake here. Discuss it with Edecón and see what he says."

"Let's talk about it at the evening meal tonight."

As the evening meal wound down and the discussion of the tin mine ended, Valencina said, "Valanin brought an unusual thought regarding Al Hued to me today. I'll let Valanin tell you what he saw."

Valanin delineated his observation of Al Hued's appearance as Shirac talked to Valencina.

"That is most disturbing," Edecón said. "Perhaps you were right, Valencina, Al Hued's intentions may not be honorable. Al Hued may be seeking a wife, or at least a plaything."

"He's looking at the wrong woman. Edecón, I am directing you to maintain contact with Shirac and Al Hued. I will not be seen by them until they are ready to leave."

"Are you accepting this challenge?" Edecón asked.

"Yes I am. Valanin suggested it for safety," Valencina said.

"Will you go to the hall of government?" Edecón asked.

"Rarely. I'll not be out and about. I'll be a prisoner here until they are ready to leave," Valencina said.

"That will be difficult for you," Edecón said.

"You will be my face to the clan until the visitors are ready to leave," Valencina said.

Valencina

"All right, I accept your decision," Edecón said.

Valanin left the next sun, feeling he had, at least, unraveled part of the mystery of the visitors.

After nearly ninety suns, the visitors from the south prepared to leave. "We wish to leave gifts to Valencina for the willingness to share what information you have on bronze. Please bring her forward," Shirac said.

Valencina entered, made a discreet bow to Al Hued and said to Shirac, "We hope we have helped you to fulfill your mission to learn about our metal works."

"You have provided all we came for and offer you these tokens of our gratitude," Shirac said.

At this point, Al Hued stepped forward and, from beneath his robe, he produced a long, curved item, resembling a horn. "This is an ivory tusk," Al Hued said, in the language of the clan. Valencina's jaw dropped, *he does understand our language. He never needed an interpreter. He is less than honest, acting as if he didn't understand us.*

Valencina accepted the tusk, smiling.

Next, Al Hued reached into the other side of his robe and extracted a flint dagger with an amber pommel. "This I offer to Edecón as a token for his unfailing assistance and negotiations of the trade agreement."

Stepping closer to Valencina, as she noticeably stiffened, he extracted two items from a third pocket in his robe. These he offered to her saying, "These I offer to you as a personal token. I'd hoped to propose marriage to you, but could not find you in time to do so. Please accept these tokens as a remembrance of me."

"That I shall do," said Valencina, with apathy yet outwardly smiling.

"We are pleased with the trade we have worked out with Edecón. I'm sure it will benefit us both," Al Hued said. "With this we will part."

"Thank you. Be safe," Valencina said, not able to squelch completely the relief in her voice.

The visitors boarded their camels and were gone.

"We will resume life as we knew it," Valencina declared.

"Yes," Edecón said, "if the trade comes about, I'll be surprised; but we are prepared if they want to honor the agreement."

"We'll see," Valencina said.

Chapter 14

An Attack Is Coming

Twelve seasons latter, a scout reported encountering a runner from a clan to the northwest. The runner's clan was under attack and near to falling. He was sent to warn other clans as he continued running to the east.

Valencina was surprised at the scout's warning and called, that sun, a meeting of her advisors. In addition, she sent a runner to Valanin to warn of impending attack.

Edecón, Daleninar and Lagunas arrived in the hall to meet with Valencina. "I have received warning from our northern scout. He will give us his report in full," Valencina said.

The scout stepped forward and began his recitation. "Early today I saw a runner approaching from the northwest. He stopped short when he saw me and, after catching his breath for a few moments he said 'I come from a clan in the north. We have been under attack from a clan much farther to the north, the Calvri people. They are planning to move south and conquer all the settlements of this land. They are bold, well equipped and unwilling to negotiate a truce. They will be here in about four seasons, if not before. I must move on.' And he was gone. I did not have time to question him, being a runner he had to move on as fast as he could."

The four governing people looked at each other, shrugging. "Who are the Calvris?" Edecón asked.

"I don't know from the north, I would guess," Valencina said.

"Maybe Valanin has heard of them," Daleninar said.

"I sent a runner to tell him of the scout report. I probably should have asked him to come down here. Maybe he'll come without my asking," Valencina said.

"I'll begin recruiting an active defense force, without slowing metal production," Edecón said.

"I'll be sure to fatten the herds and prepare to slaughter and preserve them for meat to feed the forces," Lagunas said.

I will make sure the gardens are producing as much as can be for storing for war time," Daleninar said.

Valencina

"That is good for now. We must get into planning gear without causing alarm throughout the clan. Armament production must increase, food preservation must be encouraged and the wall must be examined," Valencina said.

"I will make sure our engineers make a minute examination of the wall and shore-up any weak spots," Edecón said.

"All right, I think that's all we can do at this time," Valencina said.

The clan must be notified of the word we received from our scout. How should I do this without raising undue alarm? We must work together to prepare for this attack. That message will keep clan members focused on actions not allowing them to wallow in panic. That's the way I'll present it at a meeting in six suns, thought Valencina. *I will send a runner to Valatin to have some of their people attend also.*

Six suns later, Valencina stood before a meeting of the clan with Valanin and four other clan members from Valatin. "I called this meeting to inform you of an important message. You have probably seen and spoke with Edecón, Daleninar and Lagunas about their recruitment of warriors. Our northern scout received word from a runner from the north about an attack on a settlement nearly ready to fall. The Calvri people are determined to make inroads in the south and are heading this way. They will be here in about four seasons. I am asking you to prepare for this invasion by stockpiling food, hides and any other resources you will need. Bury your valuables and assist one another as much as possible. We will make sure the wall is repaired where needed and all animals will be secured before the attack. We will continue metal works, concentrating on armaments for all clan members, including children above the age of ten summers. Please use these next seasons to prepare to defend our settlements."

The crowd began talking among themselves and the clamor was becoming loud as some were talking ever louder to be heard. Valencina sensed an impending loss of control. She stood and invoked a prayer to the sun god, with arms raised, she began, "Oh sun god, who sees, hears and knows all, help us to prepare for an attack from the north. Watch over us with your all-seeing eyes, hear our prayer with your all-hearing ears and grant us warmth to carry on our preparations in harmony and good-will. Of this we beg of you, sun god, our god." The crowd quieted and moved to their work and their homes.

Now, the work begins. The clan knows now of the impending attack and they have the work of preparation before them. I must oversee all with the help of Edecón, Daleninar and Lagunas. We must meet in the evenings to track all preparations we can control. I will call the first meeting tonight to try to gauge how the information delivered today was received, thought Valencina.

"Daleninar, please talk to Edecón and Lagunas about a meeting tonight after the evening meal. I want to know what they're hearing from the workers of the mines, metal works and animal caretakers," Valencina said.

"I will do that, Valencina. The crowd sounded to have much disquiet about the news today," Daleninar said.

"Yes, I invoked the sun god to quiet the crowd."

"It did seem to work for the time."

"I will continue to have regular meetings, not every night but often enough to find any pockets of dissent. We need to talk to those people so the disquiet doesn't escalate."

"I agree. I'll go to find Edecón and Lagunas now and I'll visit the gardens and the cheese house."

"Thank you, Daleninar. I'll see you at the evening meal."

The evening meal was finished and Valencina opened the conversation as Lagunas came through the door, "Welcome, Lagunas. I want to begin tonight by finding any dissent among the workers you manage. Starting with Edecón, what, if anything, have you heard?"

"Well Valencina, I haven't overheard any outright dissent. A few seemed to not work quite as hard, as if their minds were elsewhere. I'll keep watching them," Edecón said.

"At the cheese house, one woman asked if there really was going to be an attack. I assured her there was. She said, 'I think Valencina just wants us to work harder to make her look better.' I asked her 'What makes you say that?' She said, 'I just think she's trying to scare us so we'll work harder then the attack won't happen and we'll have a celebration and thank the sun god.' I gave up trying to figure out what her problem was," Daleninar said.

"Thank you, Daleninar. Maybe you and I should talk with her, after she finishes work," Valencina said.

"We can but I don't think she knows what her complaint is, maybe she's just suspicious of all rulers," Daleninar said.

"That may be but something or someone must have made her think that way. I want to know more about her," Valencina said.

After Valencina nodded at Lagunas, he began, "I spoke to two of my milkers today who wanted more details about the attackers. They have relatives in the north and were concerned these people might be relatives. I told them if they attack us, they will be treated the same as any attackers. We would not know whose relative they may be. We can't drop our armaments in case someone might have a relative on the other side. That's the way wars are fought, you have to be on one side, preferably on your home side."

"That's an unusual loyalty question. You handled it well. Keep an eye on them, others may question their loyalty too, with the possibility of relatives, or just an excuse to avoid battle," Valencina said. "Keep your ears and eyes open to any disruption or slacking in work that could signal the onset of a problem. We'll meet again in five suns, unless you encounter something we all need to hear about sooner."

There seemed to be less loyalty questions as the clan settled into a pre-attack mode of hard work in preparation for the attack. Armaments, including axes, arrows and bronze arrowheads were produced in record amounts. Deer and boar were hunted and killed; the meat dried or salted for preservation. Vegetables from the gardens were dried or placed in underground cellars for future use. The copper mines were worked to prepare copper pans, bowls, pales and other useful objects to be completed into bronze, using tin from the tin mines at Valatin.

Valanin made regular visits to Valencina, Edecón, Lagunas and Daleninar to maintain regular updates and plan for the upcoming attack. Valencina maintained regular meetings of the five resulting in a plan to close the tin mine and move the entire population of Valatin to Valentin for safety and defense. In addition, Valencina decreed all mining would cease when the attack started. All effort would be channeled to defense. Valanin and Edecón would oversee armament distribution and placement of fighters on the walls and parapets. Daleninar would oversee continued milking and cheese production in the double-walled building fortified for that purpose. Scouting was increased. More scouts were sent farther afield to detect movements by the invaders.

After the entire population of Valatin was moved to Valentin and situated in appropriate housing, the settlement was full and all preparations were complete, Valencina thought, *we're as prepared as we can be. Now we must be watching for news of the invaders. Edecón and Valanin trained more scouts so we now have scouts farther north of Valatin. We should be hearing from them any sun now.*

Ten suns later, Valencina did, indeed hear from a scout. A runner arrived to relay the information from the northernmost scout who had met an escapee from the fallen clan settlement.

Breathlessly, the runner arrived in the hall of government to inform Valencina, "The clan under attack has fallen. The attackers are on the move. They will be here in about ten suns."

"Thank you," Valencina said. "Return to the scout who sent you and pass the word to recall all scouts to Valentin immediately."

I must tell Edecón to recall all the scouts and, with Valanin, begin to distribute armaments and direct placement of fighters on the walls. I will call a clan meeting to announce the anticipated attack is at hand.

Two suns later, Valencina stood before a crowd of clan members to announce the oncoming attack. "We have received a report by runner from our northernmost scout that the attackers have overwhelmed the unfortunate settlement and are now moving toward us. According to our plan, all mining operations are stopped as is metal work. The only ongoing work is milking and cheese production. Armaments are being distributed and placement of fighters is being directed by Edecón and Valanin. Lagunas and Daleninar are bringing the animals to shelter in pens behind a double wall. I will now lead a prayer to our sun god to beg for protection and victory."

Every one bowed as Valencina raised her arms to the sun and began her prayer-chant, "O mighty Sun god we are soon to be under attack. We need your help now more than ever before. You, who has given us life under your light; now we beg for freedom from the impending attack. We pray for strength to repel the invaders under your power by day. Oh Sun, shed some of your power on our fighters and make them successful warriors. For this we will thank you for the rest of our lives."

Valencina took her seat on the dais, while Edecón rose to announce the distribution of arms. "We will begin distributing arms to those of more than ten summers. Valanin will direct you to your place on the wall or as back-up. When you have the arms you need and know where you will stand, return to your homes and wait for the horn blast to call you to defend our clan and settlement." They all saluted by pumping their right fist in the air. Hearts beat faster as they chanted "Valencina, Valencina, Valencina..."

Chapter 15

The Attack

The sound of the approaching horde grew louder, howling, yelling, spears banging against bronze shields. These raiders were intent on war and destruction. The defenders populated the top of the entire wall. Valencina stood atop the wall on a parapet specifically arranged for her. All heads of the clan defenders were turned to her. She stood watching the approach of the northern horde, arm extended. When the noise of the encroaching horde reached the height of crescendo, she dropped her arm and the defenders turned and fired the first volley of arrows. The war had begun.

The horde was agitated further, attacking the front gate with rams and spears. The rams broke the gates and the spears killed the guards. The horde attempted to enter the settlement but was met by defenders who managed to push the horde back through the gate. The defenders used bows, arrows, spears, and axes to drive the horde back. They rolled logs up to the gate and, with many hands, lifted the logs to form a formidable barrier. Individuals from the horde tried to scale the logs but were shot with bronze headed arrows or skewered by bronze pointed spears. The battle at the main gate continued throughout the day. More defenders were killed on the top of the wall, some falling within the wall, some outside the wall. Nothing could be done for those falling outside the wall. The women of the clan rushed to care for the fallen within the wall. By direction of Valencina, the hall of government was opened as a caring house for the injured. The use of the bronze arrow heads by the aggressors as well as the defendants caused great suffering and resulted in lethality unknown in previous wars.

The battle continued for several more suns. Neither side showed any sign of faltering or winning. The fighting slowed to a lull after dark, to begin again at first light; each trying to take the other side by surprise. Neither side was surprised. Edecón and Valanin distributed armaments to those who needed them during the night, so the fighting forces were replenished for the coming day. As the war continued, more screams and cries sounded from the care house. The wounding impact involved penetration, with the perforation of vital organs, the release or fragmentation of the arrowhead into body tissues, infection, and radial fissures and rotation. The attempted removal of bronze arrow heads was a rare success. Bronze arrow heads were barbed so when removal was attempted the barbs anchored deeper into victim's tissue, causing increased damage and excruciating pain. Healers often refused to attempt removal of the arrowhead and treated the wound with the hope it would heal over the area, which rarely happened. Victims most often died from the damage to the tissue or infection.

The horde continued to attack the clan from outside the walls. A runner approached Valencina and breathlessly shouted, "Lagunas is dead, Daleninar commands."

Valencina nodded her appreciation. She sent the runner to Edecón saying, "Tell Edecón the news and tell him to send re-enforcements to the south wall, the animal walls."

The runner did as directed. Edecón, though, recognizing his wife was in a perilous position, motioned a group of thirty warriors held in reserve to join him on a march to the south walls, the double wall. He met Daleninar at the walls. The reserves, fresh from a rest, joined the fight and the enemy backed away. Daleninar saw this and she said to Edecón, "What a difference thirty fresh troops can make."

"I'll stay with you for a while to make sure another full attachment isn't coming," Edecón said.

"No need. You can't direct the rest of the war from here."

"I left Valanin in charge. I detect a slowing of the enemy, as if they're exhausted."

"May be but let's not relax yet."

"Yes, as long as the arrows keep coming we must fight on."

In the distance, Edecón pointed to Valencina's parapet. "There's a commotion on the parapet," he shouted.

"Yes, what is happening?"

"I'll go." Edecón left running, oblivious to any arrows coming over the wall.

He arrived some minutes later.

When he arrived, he found Valencina being treated by two guards. Her chest had been pierced by a bronze headed arrow. She moaned then stated, "Help me stand."

Standing, she said in a loud voice, louder than anybody expected "Follow Edecón."

She died in the guards' arms, as she was lowered to a carrying bed. Four men hoisted the bed and carried her body to the hall of government.

So many fighters heard her declaration to follow Edecón; they appeared to fight with more ferocity than before. Though they were unaware of the reason for the intense pronouncement, they increased their defense to save their clan and their chieftain.

Edecón sought Valanin to give him the message and make him leader of defense. Valanin would pass the message about Valencina's death to the fighters. From there, Edecón walked to Daleninar and explained about Valencina's demise. Then he found the senior member of the fighters at the wall and passed the word to follow Valanin.

Daleninar, distraught at the news, left at once to supervise the preparations of the body of Valencina. It was important all preparations be done according to family and clan leader burial traditions. Edecón arrived soon after and took control. The burial could not wait until after the war, none knew when the war would end.

"We must bury the body now," Edecón said. "The war could go on for moons."

"That we shall do then," Daleninar said.

The preparations for internment of the body required engineers to open the rock enclosure and widen an area for the body and the necessary articles to be enclosed. The gravesite looked as this drawing produced by Miriam Luciañez, University of Seville, Spain:

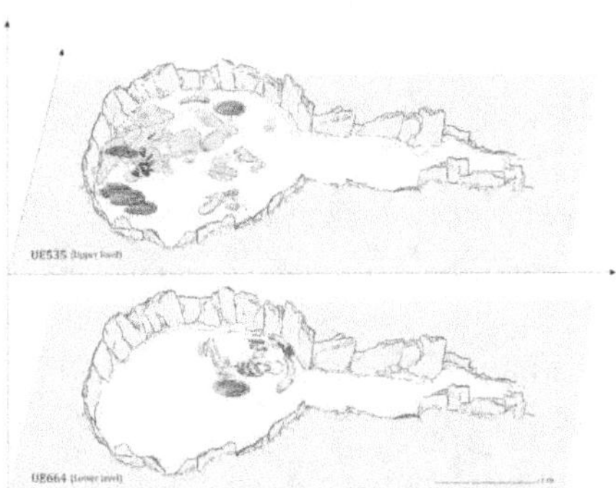

Daleninar gathered the articles to be enclosed with the body, including an ivory tusk, a comb of ivory, swords of fine metals with jewels, and ceramics—all items of importance to the living Valencina. The grave was in close proximity to her parents, other relatives and the hall of government. The entire clan would have attempted to be present for the internment but the war was of highest importance so the burial was a family affair with, Daleninar and Edecón making up the core of the small number of mourners. A larger memorial would have to wait for the war to end, which it would, in time.

Epilogue

Daleninar and Edecón returned to their posts to take up the defense of clan and settlement. The war continued for three seasons before the attackers moved away for good, leaving the wall and clan intact but with great loss of lives and severe lack of resources. Edecón followed Valencina's rule as she had made it her dying wish. He worked with Valanin and Daleninar to begin by burying the dead and mourning Valencina's death. Then they began to rebuild the clan and bring back the industries of mining and metal works. This was an arduous task because of the toll the war had taken on available, experienced workers. Time and freedom from further attack were in their favor.

The clan persisted for many more generations before it was subsumed by other clans, resulting in the loss of its independent, genetic heritage. It is now being investigated by archeologists searching the history of southern Spain. This is how the remains of the Ivory Woman were found.

About the Author

Mary Jo Nickum is an award winning author. She has published a chapter book, three young adult novels and eight reluctant reader books for high school science students.

She is a retired professional librarian and an English teacher. She lives with her husband, John, in the Phoenix, Arizona